T0106092

BARKSDALE CHRONICLES IN AMERICA, VOL I

THE STORIES OF JOHN HICKERSON AND HICKERSON BARKSDALE

ROBERT GROVES

authorHOUSE®

AuthorHouse™
1663 Liberty Drive
Bloomington, IN 47403
www.authorhouse.com
Phone: 1-800-839-8640

©2010 Robert Groves. All rights reserved.

No part of this book may be reproduced, stored in a retrieval system, or transmitted by any means without the written permission of the author.

First published by AuthorHouse 8/16/2010

ISBN: 978-1-4520-5996-9 (sc)
ISBN: 978-1-4520-5997-6 (e)

Library of Congress Control Number: 2010911299

Printed in the United States of America

This book is printed on acid-free paper.

CONTENTS

DEDICATION

To the memory of my mother, Hazel Barksdale Williamson Groves

FOREWORD

A family history cannot concentrate on just one line of descendants from generation to generation. It takes many links of siblings, children, grandchildren, aunts, uncles and cousins to place any family in its proper context. This work was started in 2000. In 2010, it is nowhere near conclusion. Instead, it is but one small snippet from the big picture of an entire family's history. This work contains a brief history of the Barksdale family prior to migration to America, William Barksdale II, the first family member to be born in America, and the descendants of his first two children, John Hickerson and Hickerson.

For those relatives who are interested, this family history contains all the information needed for successful acceptance into either the Daughters of the American Revolution or Sons of the American Revolution. Acts of Congress formed these organizations in 1896 and 1906, respectively. Their goal is to keep alive our ancestors' stories of patriotism and courage in the belief that the fight for freedom from tyranny is a universal idea.

Additionally, some relatives may be eligible for membership in the Daughters, Sons or Children of the Confederacy. As you read about your ancestors that were a part of that era, you will find that they fought on both sides during the conflict. Therefore, it is suggested that you check the requirements for membership carefully against your direct lineage. In certain cases, membership is granted if one can show a collinear link.

Finally, it is necessary to explain the unique numbering system used to identify and index each relative annotated in this history. Genealogy works typically use a descendancy line encapsulated in parenthesis immediately following each person's name as a tool for indexing. Since this work has found numerous prior generations for almost each relative, that system proved to be ineffective as well as cumbersome for the flow of readability. Therefore, a different identification and index system was developed that serves the purpose of easily locating a particular individual as well as add to the aesthetic balance sought by the author. Each bold numeral or letter preceding each relative's name represents a prior generation. For example, **II.1.2.a.1 (A) (1) John A. Doe** signifies that John is of the seventh generation with information annotated back six generations. By following the indexing system in reverse, one would be able to identify by name each of John's direct ancestors. Spouses of ancestors, while mentioned in the section for each relative, have not been indexed.

Acknowledgements

No family genealogist can accomplish a project of this magnitude without interacting with numerous people and places. Everyone and every organization that provided data to compile this volume are listed in the reference section of this history. However, the assistance of four persons has proven to be invaluable.

First, no subsequent Barksdale family history could overlook the treasure that Capt. John A. Barksdale gave us in 1940. His telling of the family history incorporated accounts from two published sources prior to his research: (1) *Genealogy of Part of the Barksdale Family of America* by Sarah Donelson Hubert in 1895 by the Franklin Printing and Publishing Company of Atlanta, GA and (2) *History-Genealogical-Biographical of the Barksdale-DuPont and Allied Families* by Walter M. Gore published in 1922 by the American Historical Society of New York. However, Capt. Barksdale found that each one covered only one particular lineage of the family pertaining to the particular author's direct descendants and he journeyed further from their endings to tie it altogether. His dedication has given us a remarkable piece of literature from which to go forward from his stopping point. While only 400 copies were printed, on occasion one can still find one available with enough patience devoted to the search. This work cites numerous pieces of data from his publication, and where new information has been found, updates his data.

Rosemary Phelan Harbin began her research on the family after her son, Chris, presented her with a gift to record her ancestry in the late 1990s. While staring at the pages and realizing she had many empty spaces, she set out to find her ancestors. During this project, she posed critical analysis to the facts that I unearthed. Her feedback has resulted in what can attest to be the most accurate portrayal possible of the family's history through today.

David J. Yost resides in Denver, Colorado. His gggggggrandmother was Lucy Barksdale, daughter of Jonathan and sibling of Nathan. His keen interest in the history surrounding the family and their activities has added a picturesque quality to this work. The credit for the history surrounding the Barksdale men's military service to this great nation and many of the tales contained herein belongs solely to him.

Finally, but certainly not least, is my sister Linda Williamson Witt. As editor extraordinaire, the huge amount of information and facts contained within flow as smooth as possible resulting in an enjoyable experience for the reader.

CHAPTER I

THE BEGINNING

The first logical question to ask and research is: Where did the name Barksdale originate? Prior to migration to America, the spelling of the surname was Barkesdale. Capt Barksdale (1940, p.4) gives a rather lengthy explanation of the history of names and naming in his book. Therefore, it is not necessary to repeat it here. What is significant is his theory that Barkesdale consists of two very succinct words: bark and dale. He writes, "In medieval England those whose occupation it was to tan hides were known as barkers as well as tanners. The name probably originated from the barkers or tanners who lived in a valley, or more probably still, the name was first given to some dale or valley wherein good bark was to be found for the tanning of hides."

Capt. John A. Barksdale found and wrote almost all of the early history of the Barksdale lineage in his 1940 book. The records of England were well-preserved allowing fairly easy genealogy research at that time. The family immigrated to Virginia from England circa 1660-1663. There they remained through the late 1660s and 1700s. However, in the 1880s, they became a rather nomadic bunch and fanned out across the United States in many directions.

This migration throughout the United States is a source of hardship on modern day researchers and there are still some inconsistencies about who went where and married whom. However, it is reasonably certain that every Barksdale of caucasian ancestry in the United States today is related through this line. For the purpose of this writing on the family's history, data sources will be provided as to what lead this researcher to reach the conclusions brought forth. Where there are differing thoughts, various viewpoints and evidence will be included so that the reader can draw his or her own conclusions or continue with further research.

In early genealogy, the first thing usually sought was a coat of arms, a crest and/or a family motto. Capt. Barksdale ruled out the existence of the latter two, but made a good argument for a coat of arms which is the only pictorial graphic in his book opposite page 12. This coat of arms is documented as being on the wall above the organ of the Worcester Cathedral as late as 1812 and believed to have been placed there by the Rev. William Barkesdale during his service of ministry from 1604 until his death in 1628. That documentation has been preserved in London in the Collections of the Society of Antiquaries (letter from organization dated 15 Jan 2003).

Per Capt Barksdale, the first mention of the name is found in England on 26 October 1332 when the Lord of the Manor of Bramley granted land to Thomas de Barkesdale and his wife, Elizabeth, for life. It is thought that Thomas took his name from a tenement then present in the Parish of Bramley. There is not another mention of the name until 5 July 1543 in the Patent Rolls where King Henry VIII granted a license to several men including a Henry Tanner alias Barkesdale.

From that time on, we find three main branches of the family - at Newbury in Berkshire, Oxford in Oxfordshire, and Winchcomb in Gloucestershire. All three branches are believed derived from Thomas de Barkesdale but their exact connections are unknown. The very first ancestor from which we can derive the present day lineage with any confidence is the Rev. William Barkesdale.

CHAPTER 2

REV. WILLIAM BARKESDALE OF THE NEWBURY BRANCH

Rev. William Barkesdale (1551-19 Feb 1628) was of the Newbury Branch. He married an unnamed cousin from the Oxford branch of the family in 1582. They had four documented children as revealed in Rev. William's will: John, Nathaniel, Richard, and Elizabeth. It is thought his wife died soon after 1618 as it is found in the records of the Cathedral of Worcester that a niece, Mary Barkesdale, kept house for him starting in 1618. (Barkesdale 1940)

Rev. William Barkesdale lived and ministered in Worcester and Hampton Counties, England. His educational and ministerial history is as follows:

Student of Christ Church College, Oxford University, 1571
BA degree July 7, 1573; MA degree Oct. 31, 1576
Vicar of Marston-St.Lawrence, Northhamptonshire, 1576
Vicar of Streatley, Berkshire 1584
Canon at St. Paul's, 1573, at Suram, 1580, at York, 1590
Prebendary (Cathedral) of Worcester 1604 to his death

John was the heir-at-law to his father's estate and therefore was the oldest child. His year of birth is estimated as 1599 as it is said he was "aged 30 and more" at the Inquisition in 1629. He went to live at the family estate at Worcester following his father's death. There is not a known spouse for him, but documentation shows that he had a son, also named John. John Jr. had a bequest from his Uncle Richard in 1630. He died circa 1701 leaving his entire estate to his cousin Barkesdale Robyns (Elizabeth's child). The bequest to his cousin leads to the conclusion John Jr. had no surviving spouse or children.

Richard was born circa 1598 and died late 1628 or very early 1629 as his will was proved on 8 February 1629. Apparently, he also had no surviving spouse or children as his estate was left to a cousin named Mary and his nephew Richard (Nathaniel's son). In Capt. Barksdale's book he is listed as a minister, but there is no ministerial history provided.

The daughter, Elizabeth, was born circa 1601 and died before 1630. She married a Robyns and they had one child, Barkesdale Robyns.

Rev. Barkesdale's other child, Nathaniel (1595-5 April 1633), followed his father into the ministry. A student first at Oxford University in 1613 but received his BA from Brasemore on 13 Dec 1615 and his MA from St. Mary's Hall 8 July 1618. Rev. Nathaniel Barkesdale was Rector of St. Martins, Worcester, England, where he is buried.

CHAPTER 3

REV. NATHANIEL BARKSDALE

Nathaniel (1595-5 April 1633), second son and child of Rev. William Barkesdale, married Dorothy Wodhull (d. 1649) at Thenford, England on 21 Nov 1622. Dorothy Wodhull was a 10th generation descendant of King Edward III of England. Her parents were Nicholas Wodhull and Barbara Hobby. They had four children: Nathaniel, Jr. born 23 May 1631 and died in infancy, Barbara (d. 1694), Richard (1625-1661) and William (1629 England-1694 VA) who is further depicted in this history as "The Emigrant".

Barbara was married to Walter Evett as proven by his will that was read on 6 December 1662. Her will was proved 8 May 1694 leaving property and personal items to cousins. Henceforth, it is assumed that she had no children.

Richard was named for his uncle. Also, apparently, he had no surviving spouse or children as his will bequeathed all his possessions to his sister Barbara.

William had a bequest from his mother, Dorothy Wodhull, in 1649 with a condition attached: "if he refrains from ills company and becomes loving and kind to his brother Richard and his sister, Barbara". Neither sibling mentions him in their wills nor do other records for William exist in England. Therefore, it is likely he never reconciled his estrangement with the family. Per Capt. Barksdale, "being the youngest son, his prospects were not bright for that particular time in England".

So, migration to the New World would have been enticing. And, there is documentation that an entire neighborhood left Winchcomb in the 1660s for Virginia. Searches of history, as well as, the various correspondences that ensued between Capt Barksdale (1940, pp. 21-27) and other parties satisfy this researcher that the ancestor mentioned in the Virginia Land Patent of 20 February 1662 is the person to which our modern day relatives can be linked.

Virginia became a colony of the English crown on 26 June 1624. The first capital was Jamestown, but following a second fire there, the capital was moved to Williamsburg. During the

Revolutionary War, the capital was moved a third time in 1780 to Richmond where it remains today. With Benedict Arnold's approach to Richmond in 1781, official records were moved to Charlottesville. During these fires and various moves, many records were either lost or destroyed. This made research difficult for persons seeking information on living souls from the years 1624 to 1780. However, the Virginia State Library has spent centuries trying to recapture some of the lost municipal records by seeking data from family bibles and other artifact. Today, that repository contains an amount of historical records second only to the Library of Congress.

CHAPTER 4

WILLIAM THE EMIGRANT

We find William, the youngest son and child of Rev Nathaniel Barkesdale and Dorothy Wodhull, listed as a head right on that land patent of February 1662. The practice at that time was for the Colony of Virginia to grant 50 acres to each individual who paid his own way to the New World or transported others. Often, expeditionary headhunters in England would gather up a group of citizens and provide them free transportation to the Colonies in exchange for their 50 acres. This is what appears to have happened with The Emigrant. The original land patent listing him, and still preserved today in the Richmond County Clerk of the Circuit Court, has 115 names and was originally issued to William Moseley and John Hull. William's name is found at page 468, column 2, and line 1 of the patent. Since a separate land grant is not found as being issued to a William Barksdale or Barkesdale, most likely William traded his 50 acres to Moseley and Hull in exchange for transportation.

Oral history, as depicted in Capt Barksdale's book, has two Barkesdale brothers expanding the family further westward into the Colony. One followed the James River and the other the Rappahannock River. Prior to 1940, some family history had it that two brothers emigrated from England, but the wills that are documented earlier prove that to be only hearsay. This author agrees with Capt Barksdale's findings from 1940 that William, son of Rev. Barkesdale and Dorothy Wodhull, arrived in Virginia circa 1660-1663, married, probably died a short time after marriage and left two sons. One son, also known as William and married a Miss Collier and the other son, given name unknown, who married Sarah Daniel account for the tradition of the family in America. This son William is depicted henceforth in this history as William II. Other oral history states that "The Emigrant" took ill on the voyage from England to America and died shortly after his arrival leaving a pregnant wife alone in the new land. No documentary proof as to that story has been located.

Upon arrival, the spelling of the family name changed from Barkesdale to Barksdale. No documentation exists for why a name change occurred. The reason may be as simple as pronunciation. The phonetic spelling of Barksdale is more in keeping than Barkesdale. However, if William the Emigrant did leave England estranged from his immediate family, then the name change may have been an act of rebellion to disassociate him with them. Whatever the reason, the present day spelling has remained in all documents since records dating back to William II.

CHAPTER 5

THE LINEAGE OF WILLIAM BARKSDALE II

William II (1695-1771), became the first Barksdale ancestor to be born, live and die in the New World. He married Sarah Collier and together they had seven children: John Hickerson, Hickerson, Collier, Thomas Henry, William, Daniel, and Nathaniel. It is from these seven contemporary Barksdale men that the family grew. The census records, as well as the records of the Virginia State Library, that have became available since Capt. Barksdale's publication in 1940 have lead to the discovery of so much more from this point. In the 1940 publication, none of the dates of birth were known for any of their children and sparse information was available on their spouses and children. Modern day research now leads to the conclusion that John Hickerson was "John" in the 1940 book and that the "Thomas" mentioned briefly at the end of section III is actually part of the information belonging to "Henry," thus Thomas Henry. If any information is thought suspect from the 1940 book it would be that a separate "Hickerson" Barksdale existed, as of the seven contemporaries, his is the only will that has not been located.

All of these gentlemen were interacting in the same area of Virginia at the same time. They were purchasing and selling land, bringing court actions, witnessing each other's deeds, standing as guarantors on bonds, and acting as executors and guardians for those deceased. But as Barksdale pointed out in 1940, in genealogy, the further in years one goes back for information, the more apt mistakes are to follow as records become lost, rewritten and translated differently from the original. There is no absolute certainty beyond three to four generations removed unless we discipline ourselves to better record keeping. That no one, knowingly, has published additional writings since the 1940 history is a telltale sign in itself of our indolence with preserving data.

CHAPTER 6

II.1. JOHN HICKERSON BARKSDALE (CIRCA 1710 VIRGINIA – 1796 ABBEVILLE COUNTY, SC)

Parents: William Barksdale II and Sarah Collier

The first documentary evidence of John Hickerson is from 1755 where he bought a tract of land in Lunenburg County, a part of which later became Charlotte County. This land was located adjacent to Butterwood and Rattlesnake Creeks, east of the Blue Ridge Mountains.

Approximately September 1774, he closed out his land ownership and in October 1774 refused to act as an executor for his brother Collier. Some historians have concluded this meant he was getting ready to leave. So, we ask, leave for where? And, the answer is South Carolina. There is documentation in the history of Virginia the colony of John Caldwell migrated from there to South Carolina in the latter part of 1774 and early part of 1775. How long that migration took is anyone's guess, but there are no land records for him in South Carolina until 1785.

In the South Carolina State Archives in Columbia, the following grants of land are found from the Ninety-Six District.

03 October 1785 John Barksdale 248 acres

07 November 1785 John Barksdale 200 acres

03 October 1785 Hickson Barksdale 228 acres

07 March 1791 Daniel Barksdale 127 acres

02 February 1795 Allen Barksdale 110 acres

03 October 1796 Higgarson Barksdale 25 acres

06 November 1797 Hickeson Barksdale 342 acres

03 December 1798 Hickerson Barksdale, Jr 279 acres

The Ninety-Six District, at that time, included the counties of Abbeville, Edgefield, Greenville, Laurens, Newberry, Pendleton, Spartanburg, and Union. In the first U.S. census of 1790, John was in Abbeville County along with Hickerson, Richard and Allen. Additionally, William

Barksdale was in Laurens County, and his brother Daniel and nephew Joseph was in Edgefield County.

From court documents of May 1785, John Hickerson had a wife named Mary Anne Kinkaid. Copies examined in Abbeville County, SC show she filed to relinquish her right to the land John had sold in Charlotte County, VA on 06 September 1774 due to being apart from said John Barksdale. "The certificate of acknowledgment in May 1785 is conclusive that she was living in Abbeville, and she was evidently dead by Dec 1790 when John wrote his will." (Young, 1950) Marriage documents in Halifax County, VA, show they were married in May 1754.

There were eight named children in his will on file in the Abbeville County, SC Probate Court: Thomas, Anna, Cleavers, Unity Nancy, Richard, Polly, Frances, and Hickerson or Higgason.

John Hickerson is interred in Abbeville County, SC. From information in his will, he married a second time, post 1790, to a Susanna Cowan. She signed a written statement relinquishing her right to administer on her husband's estate on 9 September 1796. Her brother, James Cowan, was a signatory to that statement. The children of John and Unity Martin finally probated the will on 19 October 1807 for a total of $5,000, according to the settlement sheet contained within the file.

Chapter 7

II.1.a. Thomas Barksdale = (d. before 28 Apr 1784)

Parents: John Hickerson Barksdale and Mary Anne Kinkaid

Thomas definitely pre-deceased his father, as John Hickerson's will lists him as being so. The will also shows he was granted 250 acres at some point and his father claimed that property as the executor of Thomas' estate, along with his slaves. Nothing in the records indicates a spouse or other heirs until one reads John Hickerson's will. In his will is the phrase: "Secondly, I will to my Beloved Son Thomas Barksdale one Negro woman named Mary and her children to be divided amongst his heirs." Those heirs are not mentioned by name.

CHAPTER 8

II.1.B. ANNA BARKSDALE

Parents: John Hickerson Barksdale and Mary Anne Kinkaid

According to her father's will she was married twice. Her first marriage was to Ben Davis as the will specifically gives 100 acres of land to her to be divided equally to her five children by Ben Davis upon her death. However, in the will she is annotated as Anna Davis Williamson.

Per *Martins of Martin's Mill of South Carolina*, p. 31: "Anna Barksdale married 1st Benjamin Davis, had issue of five children, married 2nd Williamson and had issue." To this date, the names of those children remain unknown.

CHAPTER 9

II.1.c. CLEAVERS BARKSDALE (1746 CHARLOTTE COUNTY, VA-BEFORE 4 AUGUST 1784)

Parents: John Hickerson Barksdale and Mary Anne Kinkaid

He also had died prior to his father, who along with Unity's spouse, John Martin, Sr., were the executors of his will. John Hickerson left Cleavers' daughter, Patsy, one Negro man named Will.

Cleavers Barksdale is shown as owning land near Matthew Talbot II in the Watauga area.

He married Mary Talbot (1753 Bedford County, VA-?) on 24 May 1772 in Bedford County, VA. They had the one daughter, Patsy.

II.1.c.a. PATSY BARKSDALE

Parents: Cleavers Barksdale and Mary Talbot

John White (2000) claims, "that Mary Talbot Barksdale had only one child, Patsy, who married her first cousin, a Barksdale. She later married Cal Adams and died in Alabama."

[http://www.geocities.com/fww64/mt_II.html, 2000]

CHAPTER 10

II.1.d. UNITY NANCY BARKSDALE

Parents: John Hickerson Barksdale and Mary Anne Kinkaid

As will be found throughout the family history, the female lines are stronger. This is certainly true for Unity's line; the first substantial Barksdale lineage in America.

The records contain a settlement sheet from John Martin, Sr, guardian to legatees of John Barksdale, set forth in pounds, shillings and pence and then converted into American dollars, and were filed Oct. 19, 1807. The legatees named were William Martin, John Martin, Polly Freeman and Sally David, children of John Martin and his wife, Unity Barksdale. John Matheson, Adm., John Martin and Joshua Hill, Nov. 7, 1796 for $5,000 signed Bond. Receipts signed by Joseph Barksdale; William, son of John Martin; John, son of John Martin; James Freeman and wife, Polly; and Isaac David and wife, Sally. (Abbeville Co., Box 104; Packs 2632; 2666)

According to her father's will Unity married John Martin (1731 VA-Dec. 1821 Abbeville, SC). From the probate of Unity's father's will in 1807, their children were: William (b. 1783 Abbeville, SC), John Jr. (1780 Abbeville, SC-1842 Edgefield, SC), Polly *a.k.a. Mary* (3 July 1784 Edgefield, SC-7 January 1859 Abbeville County, SC), and Sally (b. 1785 SC).

While data is lacking as to the marriage of John Martin, Sr and Unity Barksdale, it is probable that they were married soon after he settled in South Carolina [subsequent research has learned that John Martin first came to SC in about 1756, returned to VA to marry his first wife whom he brought back with him to SC. Obviously, he married Unity after the death of his first wife]. It will be remembered that John Barksdale's plantation and ferry were only a few miles away from Martin's home site, and Martin was perhaps a widower in search of a suitable companion. While it is only guesswork, John and Unity may have met at the meeting house [church], which was midway between their homes. In any event they were married and were the parents of four children, all of whom were heirs to the estate of their grandfather, John Barksdale in the early 1800s, their mother Unity having passed away. In passing it may be mentioned that John Barksdale remarried, his wife by that marriage having been Susannah Cowan. (Young)

John Martin purchased land on 1 Oct 1771 in Broad River, SC. He is listed in the 1780 census of Kershaw District, SC. He is interred at McCormick, SC. His will is on file at Abbeville County, South Carolina Clerk of Probate Court (Box 59, Pkg. 1399)

II.1.d.a. John Martin, Jr. (1780 Abbeville, SC-1842 Edgefield County, SC)

Parents: John Martin Sr. and Unity Nancy Barksdale

He married Abigail Freeman (1785 SC-10 May 1863 Edgefield County, SC) in 1803 in Edgefield County, SC. John Martin Jr. in 1803 purchased 98 acres on Westcoat's Creek about 10 miles from his father's place, located just over the county line between Abbeville and Edgefield counties. He bought this land from Andrew Willis for $300. Newby, Willis, and Roden bound it. In August 1806 he sold the same to Wells and in November 1806 he purchased another tract of 150 acres for $300 from Jesse Parker. This also was located on Westcoat's Creek. Witnesses were James Freeman and Baugh.

A copy of his will is found in the office of Probate Judge, Edgefield County, SC. (Box 50, Pkg. 2139) The couple had six known children and two unnamed female children. Abigail's will refers to two predeceased daughters. Their children were: Beatrice, Patsy, Toliver Pinkney (Dec 1814 SC-before 1863), Asbury (b. 1809 SC), James Franklin (24 March 1810 SC-5 November 1880 Clay County, AL), and Elizabeth (b. 16 December 1818 SC). Per information pieced together from both John Jr.'s and Abigail's will, one of the predeceased daughters married Isaac Caldwell and had a son named William.

In the 1850 census of Clay Co AL, Abigail Freeman is listed in the household of James F. Martin and as being born in 1785.

Young writes, "Substantiation evidence of relationship is found in mortgage of place where John Martin Jr. lived, given by his wife, Abigail Martin, to her children as security for their help in paying debt to Thomas Ferguson. It reads in part: 31 Dec 1842, Abigail Martin and N S Matthews (Mathis), Elizabeth Martin, Toliver Martin, Isaac Caldwell, James F Martin and Beatrice Martin . . . District of Edgefield, SC . . . $1422.51 debt to Thomas Ferguson . . . hath agreed to convey all her interest in the tract of land whereon she now lives. Personal estate consisting of four likely Negroes . . . mare and colt, 15 head hogs, 2 cows and calves, all household and kitchen furniture etc. Recorded 9 Jan 1843. Witnesses: Book CCC, p. 196 Clerk of Court, Edgefield CH."

"In 1858 Abigail deeded to my granddaughter, Martha Palmer wife of Ninean Palmer, an infant slave." (Young, p. 40)

Abigail died intestate on May 10, 1863 and in the petition of Milton J Palmer, her son-in-law, for Letters of Administration stated she left the following children: Asbury Martin (Littleberry had been scratched through and Asbury written above it); James F. Martin; Patsy Mathis wife of Newman Mathis; Beatrice Palmer, wife of Dale C. Palmer; Eliza wife of Milton J. Palmer; and grandchildren, Martha, wife of Ninean Palmer, child of a pre-deceased daughter; William Caldwell, child of another pre-deceased daughter; and the children of Toliver Martin, pre-deceased son, names unknown. Value of the estate as of August 15, 1863, after paying J. F. Martin his part, was $1075.00. (Edgefield County Probate Records Box 88, Pkg. 3548)

II.1.D.A.1. BEATRICE MARTIN (1823 SC-?)

Parents: John Martin, Jr. and Abigail Freeman

1850 census: Abbeville County, SC married to Palmer; annotated age 27.

1860 census: Coosa County, AL married to Palmer and 6 children; annotated age 38; Dale's occupation was listed as farmer.

She married Dale C. Palmer (13 August 1821 Edgefield, SC-?) in 1847. Per the 1860 census, they had six children: Carolina, Pauline, Amenett, unreadable female child name, Gertrude, and Eugene.

Beatrice is mentioned in her mother's will of 1863.

II.1.D.A.2. PATSY MARTIN

Parents: John Martin, Jr. and Abigail Freeman

She married Newman S. Mathis. Their marriage is substantiated through Newman's father's will. His parents were of the Quaker religion. Patsy is mentioned in her mother's will of 1863.

II.1.D.A.3. TOLIVER PINKNEY MARTIN (DEC 1814 SC-BEFORE 1863)

Parents: John Martin, Jr. and Abigail Freeman

He married Rebekah Whitney and removed to Barnwell County, SC. (Young, p.39)

His children are mentioned as heirs in his mother's will who died 10 May 1863. However, the specific names of the children are not listed.

Rebekah's father's will of 31 October 1827 lists him and Rebekah as heirs.

At the time this family was going strong in Barnwell, now Aiken County, Eli Whitney was in the next county inventing the cotton gin.

At this point in history, the Great Migration into the Mississippi Territory began and many of the Martin relatives joined the move west. Adventurous settlers, anxious to improve their fortunes, took up new lands in the west, confidently expecting them to be better than the lands they left behind. Westward movement of the colonists continued throughout the 17th and 18th centuries. By the time they declared their independence from Britain in 1776, Americans had pushed the line of settlement westward to the Appalachian Mountains.

After the Revolution, the westward movement of Americans intensified. In 1800 there were only two states west of the Appalachians — Kentucky and Tennessee. In 1820 there were eight: Kentucky, Tennessee, Ohio, Louisiana, Illinois, Indiana, Mississippi, and Alabama. The population of these areas had grown from 386,000 persons in 1800 to 2,216,000 in 1820. (Sansing 1999, p.53)

The Mississippi country was opened to settlement in 1798 when Congress organized the Mississippi Territory. Until it became a separate territory in 1817, Alabama was part of Mississippi. A few settlers already lived in Mississippi when it became a territory. They were concentrated in two principal areas — the Natchez District and the lower Tombigbee settlements above and west of Mobile. Approximately 4,500 people, including slaves, lived at Natchez, considerably more than the combined free and slave population of 1,250 that inhabited the Tombigbee settlements in 1800. Outside of these two areas, only Native Americans populated the land. (Owen 1921, p. 17)

Immigrants coming into the territory could expect none of the conveniences or comforts of the civilized world they left behind. The deprivation and hardship that awaited the immigrant in the raw, primitive Mississippi wilderness of 1800 raises a fundamental question: Why would a person choose to leave the comfort and convenience of an established farm in one of the older communities for the perilous uncertainty of life in the Mississippi wilds? The answer to this question, in a word, is — Opportunity.

For the average person, economic opportunities had diminished in the older southern agricultural states as the available supply of fertile land dwindled. Generations of ruinous agricultural practices had, by 1800, exhausted the soils of the old plantations. This made the rich virgin land of Mississippi all the more attractive. The decline in soil fertility of the upper South had been accompanied by a sharp decrease in demand for tobacco, the region's staple product. (Owen, p.13)

After the Revolution, the decline in European demand for tobacco and rice caused anxiety among southern farmers. In the 1790s, the invention of the cotton gin, together with a sharp rise in the foreign demand for southern cotton, created outstanding economic opportunities for southern farmers and fueled the Great Migration. The rich soils of the Mississippi Territory, its favorable environment for cotton culture, and the high prices being paid in England for cotton led to the genesis of the Cotton Kingdom. Mississippi, with soil and climate ideally suited to growing cotton, became the center of the nation's cotton production during the first half of the 19th century. (Owen, p. 37)

Closely linked to the notion that Mississippi offered exceptional economic opportunities for the immigrant was the widespread belief that the territory was an idyllic" "Garden of Eden," an unlimited expanse of fertile country "like the land of promise, flowing with milk and honey."

One Mississippi immigrant described his new home as "a wide empty country with a soil that yields such noble crops that any man is sure to succeed." Another new settler wrote to his family back in Maryland that "the crops [here] are certain... and abundance spreads the table of the poor man and contentment smiles on every countenance." (Owen, p. 54)

Thousands of immigrants moved to the Mississippi Territory believing they were taking up residence in a land of unsurpassed opportunity. Hard work and resourcefulness were sure to be rewarded with prosperity, security, and happiness. For white Americans, though certainly not for black slaves, Mississippi symbolized the promise of American life.

During the first phase of the Great Migration, which began in 1798 and continued until 1819, two distinct waves of immigrants swept into the Territory. The first wave began when the Territory was organized and subsided when the War of 1812 began. The second wave developed after the war ended in 1814. It peaked in the years 1818-1819 and receded after the Panic of 1819 brought about a general economic depression. In the period from 1798 to 1812, the flow of immigrants was steady but unspectacular, at least by comparison with the 1815-1819 period. In the first period, settlers moved primarily into three general areas — the Natchez country, the lower Tombigbee River basin, and the Tennessee Valley.

After 1814, immigration surpassed anything that ever had been witnessed. Thousands of immigrants began to pour into the country. By horse, by wagon, by boat, and on foot, the flood of humanity swept into the Territory. One traveler, during nine days of travel in 1816, counted no fewer than 4,000 immigrants coming into the Territory. Residents of the older states, such as Virginia and the Carolinas, began to fear the "Mississippi Fever" would depopulate their states. Everyone seemed to be moving to Mississippi. (Owen, p. 87)

In 1819 an economic panic, followed by a general depression, arrested the flood of migration. But by that time enough immigrants had settled in the country to allow both Mississippi and Alabama to come into the Union as new states — Mississippi in 1817 and Alabama in 1819. The Alabama portion of the Territory grew even more during the 10 years, increasing the population 16 fold. In 1810, 6,422 whites and 2,624 slaves lived in the Alabama section of the Territory. In 1820, those numbers had grown to 99,198 whites and 47,665 slaves, an increase of 137,817 persons. (Statistics provided by the University of Alabama at Birmingham.)

II .1.D.A.4 ASBURY MARTIN (1809 SC-1851 MONTGOMERY, AL)

Parents: John Martin, Jr. and Abigail Freeman

Asbury was the first of his family to move westward into Alabama in the 1830s. He chose to settle around Montgomery prior to it becoming the state capital. The legislature held its first session there December 6, 1847 (Owen, p. 11).

Montgomery County has a very colorful background. Settlers first began to populate the area in the early 1800s. The county of Montgomery was created by an Act of the Legislature of the Mississippi Territory on December 6, 1816. It was carved out of Monroe County and originally embraced the whole of central Alabama, east of the ridge dividing the Tuscaloosa and Tombigbee

Rivers from the Cahaba River, west of the Okfuskee and Coosa, and south of the mountains of Blount. However, it was soon subdivided and portions were set apart which made up Elmore, Bullock, and Crenshaw counties. (Owen, p. 17)

The lands of Montgomery County were put up for auction at the Federal Land Office in Milledgeville, Georgia in 1816. Larger parcels were sold to developers who subdivided the land into lots for urban commercial and residential use, predetermining a major city on the banks of the Alabama River at Montgomery. (Owen, p. 19)

A hardy class of people penetrated the wilderness. Settlements and towns sprang into existence everywhere. The City of Montgomery, which became the county seat in 1822, was built on the side of the Indian town Ikanatchati (Econachatee), which means red ground, and Towasa on a high red bluff known to Alibamu Indians as Chunnaanaauga Chatty. (Owen, pp. 21-22)

When the Alabama Lands were offered for sale in 1817, two groups of speculators made their initial payments. One group, a company of Georgians led by General John Scott, bought the area along the river bluff and called it "Alabama Town." Later, a second group, led by Andrew Dexter, bought the area bounded by present day Court, Ripley, Scott, and Jefferson Streets and named it "New Philadelphia." The Georgians abandoned the Alabama Town and built the town of East Alabama, in competition. A bitter rivalry between the two groups was finally terminated when the two towns were merged under the name Montgomery. The city was incorporated December 3, 1819, 11 days before Alabama was admitted into the Union. (Owen, pp. 31-33)

Asbury Martin was married two times having children by his second wife only. First spouse was Elizabeth Johnston (b. 1790 Montgomery, AL) and they were wed on 17 January 1832. His second spouse was Alice Hedgepath (1820 Robeson County, NC-20 August 1849 Montgomery, AL). They were wed on 28 September 1841 in Montgomery and had two children: Zachariah M. (1 May 1845 Montgomery, AL-25 January 1892 Smith County, TX) and Henry "Hobbie" (13 January 1849 Montgomery, AL-24 October 1906 Montgomery, AL).

Asbury's wife, Alice, died eight months after the birth of Henry Martin in August 1849. Asbury died in 1851, leaving the children orphaned. A family friend, Rebecca Hobbie of Montgomery, took in Henry Martin and raised him. He later became Henry Martin Hobbie.

Asbury is mentioned in his mother's will of 1863. Since Asbury had died in 1851, it is assumed his mother must have written the will between 1843 and 1851 and never revised it.

II.1.d.a.4.a Zachariah Martin (1 May 1845 Montgomery, AL-25 Jan 1892 Smith County, TX)

Parents: Asbury Martin and Alice Hedgepath

While Asbury's second son, Henry Martin Hobbie, remained in the Montgomery area and made quite a prosperous living, his first son, Zachariah, was more adventuresome and moved to Texas around the area of Kaufman and Smith counties. Perhaps the death of both parents early in life gave Zachariah a sense of freedom to move on to another geographical location.

Zachariah was the Justice of Peace for Covington County, AL for a short time. He married Sarah L. "Pup" Stanley (19 October 1844 Troup County, GA-1 February 1890 Smith County, TX) on 31 August 1865 at Pike County, AL. They had 10 children: Mary Alice "Allie" (9 September 1866 Pike County, AL0-21 August 1947 Houston, TX), Cora Eugenia (28 February 1868 AL-15 September 1872 AL), Josephine "Jodie" Ardella (24 December 1869 AL-15 October 1923 Smith County, TX), Rosa Lee Anna (30 January 1872 AL-1939 Midland, TX), William Monroe (23 September 1873 AL-6 May 1917 Smith County, TX), Nora Ella (22 August 1875 AL-August 1960 CA), Andrew Alfred (8 September 1877 Covington County, AL-17 November 1962 Smith County, TX), twins Nancy Eunis (26 April 1879 AL-2 July 1962 Houston, TX) and Sarah Frances (26 April 1879 AL-14 July 1879 AL), and Sherman Fielder (7 April 1885 AL-23 January 1926 Henderson County, TX).

Zachariah served through the entire Civil War as a private in the Confederate Army company organized in Pike County, AL.

The City of Kaufman, county seat of Kaufman County Texas, is the oldest community in the area of the "Three Forks" of the Trinity River which has been continuously inhabited. The "Three Forks" (West Fork, Elm Fork, and East Fork) region was known as a rich, fertile area which served as an Indian hunting ground and, at the end of the 1830s, contained the largest Indian village east of the Brazos River.

The way for prospective settlers in this area was blocked by the "Cherokee Lands"- territory assigned to the Cherokee, Kickapoo, and Shawnee Indians by the Mexican government. The present Kaufman County, then a part of the Nacogdoches County, lay just to the west of the northern end of the Cherokee Lands. The new Republic of Texas under its first President, Sam Houston honored this early agreement for several years despite pressure from land-hungry settlers. Finally, a new President, Mirabeau Lamar, using complaints of attacks and thefts by the Cherokees as his reason, ordered them to move beyond the Red River. They refused, but lost a decisive battle in July 1839 in which their leader, Chief Bowles, was killed. They were then driven out of their lands. This opened the way for settlement, but there were still many Indians there who were able, for a while, to intimidate those willing to venture into this northern area.

Dr. William P. King, an entrepreneur from Mississippi, had come to Texas earlier in 1839 as president of the Southern Land Company. This company had purchased Texas land script ("Toby Script") entitling the holder to locate and own land. This script had been sold by Sam Houston to raise money for the fledgling republic. Following the defeat of Chief Bowles, King signed a contract in August 1839 with Warren A. Ferris to survey over 400,000 acres (90 leagues and labors) in the "Three Forks." The following month, Ferris began the first of several unsuccessful attempts to reach the region, but each time was turned back by Indian attacks or threats of attack. Finally, on June 3, 1840, Ferris and King left Nacogdoches with 29 men. Despite the dryness of the season ("water was to be found only in holes"), over 500,000 acres of land was surveyed for King and others in June and July by three teams led by deputy surveyors, one of whom was the young Robert A. Terrell. Terrell was destined to play an important role in the country's history.

Another surveyor who worked with Ferris in 1840 was John H. Reagan, a man who was to play an even larger role in the history of the state and nation.

On Ferris's return to Nacogdoches in early August, he wrote, "...Thousands of occasional bear would sometimes cross our path. The prairies are boundless and present a beautiful appearance, being extremely fertile and crowned with flowers of every hue..."

Following the completion of the survey, King established his headquarters on the present site of the City of Kaufman. He built a stockade called King's Fort on a bluff overlooking a creek now called King's Creek. This stockade consisted of four cabins surrounded by pickets, enclosing about three-quarters of an acre. The pickets were formed of poles only a few inches in diameter and 10 feet long, set about two feet in the ground. A garrison of only 10 or 12 men at times defied the whole Indian force of that section and sustained their position with as little difficulty as if walls and battlements of massive stone protected them.

Robert Terrell related the story of one attack in which the gate of the fort had been left open and only four men were in the fort. The barking of a watchdog gave the men a warning of danger and they saw about 30 Indians riding rapidly toward the gate. The gate was shut just in time and the Indians wheeled around, rode a short distance, and held a discussion. They then galloped back for an attack, but Terrell shot the lead horse in the forehead. As the rider fell, an Indian companion pulled him up on his horse. The Indians then gave up the attack, but stole the four horses belonging to the men in the fort. To the surprise of the men seemingly now stranded, seven horses stolen by the Indians at an earlier time in Red River County were left grazing nearby. They were quickly driven into the fort, and thus a profitable exchange was made.

During the summer of 1841, Dr. William P. King took Judge John H. Martin of Vicksburg, Mississippi on a tour of his property. Judge Martin was so favorably impressed with the country he decided to join Dr. King and settle in Texas. Dr. King and Judge Martin started for Mississippi. Dr. King was to visit his family at Holly Springs and to prepare for their move to Texas and Judge Martin headed to Vicksburg to arrange for his family to move to Texas also.

However, both men contracted yellow fever on their journey and died within a few days of each other sometime during the week of September 18, 1841. Adolphus Sterne of Nacogdoches wrote in his diary "Friday the 8th of October...news was received that Dr. King, the founder of Kingsborough, and Judge Martin, who lately visited this country, died at Vicksburg or on the River Mississippi of yellow fever. This is a great loss to this part of Texas. Dr. King was an enterprising man and the country near the Three Forks of the Trinity will be thrown back at least five years - unless some very strong effort is made by his heirs or successors to carry on the work which he began." (Excerpts taken from Wilbarger, 1889 and Kaufman GenWeb Project)

II.1.D.A.4.A (1) MARY ALICE "ALLIE" MARTIN (9 SEP 1866 PIKE COUNTY, AL-21 AUG 1947 HOUSTON, TX)

Parents: Zachariah Martin and Sarah L. "Pup" Stanley

She married James Appleton Haygood (18 July 1864 Pike County, AL-8 August 1930 Harris County, TX) on 19 November 1882 at Covington County, AL.

They are located in the 1920 federal census in Kaufman County, TX. His occupation is listed as a laborer and they have six children in the house with them: William Z., Dwight L., Homer H., Eunice, Clifford, and Monroe. According to the 1930 census they are residing in the residence of Clifford at Houston, Texas. Mary is annotated as "Allie".

II.1.D.A.4.A (1) (A) WILLIAM ZACHARIAH HAYGOOD (2 JANUARY 1899 SMITH COUNTY, TEXAS-8 AUGUST 1989 KAUFMAN COUNTY, TEXAS)

Parents: James Appleton Haygood and Mary Alice Martin

William applied for a Social Security card in 1956 while living in Terrell, TX. There is a William F. Haygood listed in Commanche County, TX in the 1930 census. The age matches but the middle initial is "F" and the birthplaces of the parents do not match. His Social Security Administration records clearly have his middle initial as "Z" as does the 1920 census.

I.1.D.A.4.A (1) (B) DWIGHT L. HAYGOOD (15 JULY 1901 TEXAS-24 OCTOBER 1980 KAUFMAN, TX)

Parents: James Appleton Haygood and Mary Alice Martin

He is found in the 1930 census at Houston, Texas in residence of his brother Clifford with occupation listed as a tool machinist and single. Dwight eventually married Mary Margaret Zimmerman (d. 02 February 1996 Potter County, TX) of Cass County, TX. They had two sons: Lloyd Ware and David Carrol. (England, 1965)

II.1.D.A.4.A (1) (C) HOMER HOWARD HAYGOOD (1904 TEXAS-25 JULY 1997 HARRIS COUNTY, TX)

Parents: James Appleton Haygood and Mary Alice Martin
The only records located other than the 1920 census has been his Social Security Administration records.

II.1.D.A.4.A (1) (D) EUNICE HAYGOOD (1905 TEXAS-?)

Parents: James Appleton Haygood and Mary Alice Martin
She is located in the 1930 census at Houston, Texas in the residence of her brother, Clifford. Occupation was listed as stenographer for a real estate company; single.

II.1.D.A.4.A (1) (E) HENRY CLIFFORD HAYGOOD (4 SEPTEMBER 1908 KAUFMAN COUNTY, TX- 01 NOVEMBER 1981 HUTCHINSON, TX)

Parents: James Appleton Haygood and Mary Alice Martin
He is found through the 1930 census to be in Houston, Texas where he owned a home with an estimated value of $4500. Many of his family members were residing with him. His occupation is listed as a tool machinist and he remains single. From his Social Security Administration records we discover that in 1936 he was working for Cameron Iron Works in Houston.

Clifford married first time Selsor Gay Rudy (31 October 1913- 19 August 1995 Hutchinson, TX). They had the following children: Gerald, Michael, F. Don, Kenneth, Tanya, and Brian. (England)

His second wife was Mary Lou O'Rear whom he married 2 July 1956. They had one daughter, Donna Ruth. (England)

Gerald was residing in Dallas, Texas as of 18 November 2000. Michael was residing in Fort Worth, Texas as of 18 November 2000. Don was a practicing physician in Tyler, TX as of 18 November 2000. No additional information has been located for Tanya and Brian. Donna Ruth married Kerry Darrell Sarchet and was residing in Tarrant County, TX as of 18 November 2000. (Reynolds, 2003)

II.1.d.a.4.a (1) (F) Monroe Haygood (b. 1893 Texas)

Parents: James Appleton Haygood and Mary Alice Martin
  He has no further documented records after the 1920 census.

II.1.d.a.4.a (2) Cora Eugenia Martin (28 February 1868 AL-15 September 1872 AL)

Parents: Zachariah Martin and Sarah L. "Pup" Stanley
  Having died at the age of 4 years, no further records exist.

I.1.d.a.4.a (3) Josephine Ardella Martin (24 December 1869 AL-15 October 1923 Smith County, TX)

Parents: Zachariah Martin and Sarah L. "Pup" Stanley
  She was never married and is interred at Mount Sylvan in Smith County, TX.

II.d.a.4.a (4) Rosa Lee Anna Martin (30 January 1872 AL-1939 Midland, TX)

Parents: Zachariah Martin and Sarah L. "Pup" Stanley
  She married Reeves Young Barron (17 April 1867-4 June 1916) on 8 December 1890 in Smith County, TX. Reeves' descendants lived in the Midland, TX area. He and his two brothers, John and James, were very successful businessmen and ranchers in that region.
  In the 1920 census, Rosa is located in Midland, Texas with occupation listed as a housekeeper in the residence of Henry Cummings and widowed. A 1930 census listing was not found.

II.d.a.4.a (5) William Monroe Martin (23 September 1873 Covington AL-6 May 1917 Smith County, TX)

Parents: Zachariah Martin and Sarah L. "Pup" Stanley
  William Monroe found Smith County a better place to inhabit than Kaufman County. Like Kaufman County, the forced removal of the Indians from East Texas in 1839 opened the area for

Anglo settlement. At first, a few entrepreneurs moved in to take over the numerous salines, or salt works, formerly operated by the Indians. Later, settlers began clearing farms. During the years of the Republic of Texas, the entire area comprised part of Nacogdoches County. Smith County was one of several new counties formed by the new Texas state legislature in April of 1846.

The county grew rapidly in population and wealth throughout the decade that preceded the Civil War, with a large portion of the population emigrating from Alabama. Smith County began the 1850's with a population of 4,292, of whom 717 were Negro slaves (1850 federal census). Agriculture remained dominant in Smith County throughout the 19th century with cotton and other products reaching markets by flatboat down the Sabine River from Belzora or by ox-drawn wagon to Jefferson and Shreveport. Light frontier industries were established, including several flour and gristmills, and shops for making wagons, spinning wheels, cabinets, and guns.

Following the Civil War, Smith County began another period of rapid agricultural growth that continued through the turn of the century. Though hundreds of Smith County soldiers lost their lives to bullets or disease during the war, the conflict brought economic development rather than the wholesale destruction common throughout much of the South. Railroads arrived in Smith County in the 1870's, including the "Tyler Tap Railroad" which granted access to the Texas and Pacific Railway in 1877. This rapid, economical transportation link marked the beginning of a new industrial age for Smith County and coincided with the official end of Reconstruction.

William married Mertie Alma Pool (17 September 1877 Smith County TX-31 August 1956 Smith County, TX) on 28 November 1898 in Smith County, TX. Martha Dingler Moore, granddaughter, shares: "He died from pneumonia after a horse had dragged him on May 6. He was going to ride the horse from the field, got on and his foot became tangled in trace chains and then the horse got scared and ran dragging him all the way to the house, then just stood still until someone could come and take the harness off. He never regained consciousness. They lived on a farm - had fruit - mainly strawberries, peaches, blackberries, pears and apples - they did have vegetables also".

Their children listed in the 1920 census were Mary E., Sarah E., William R. Jeff M., and Margaret F. Mertie is widowed and working as a saleswoman in a grocery store. Her mother, Mary E. Barron is also annotated as residing in the residence. In the 1930 census she remained in Smith County, TX working as a seamstress from her home. Information on both William and Mertie is listed in the Church of the Latter Day Saints (LDS) archives.

II.1.D.A.4.A (5) (A) MARY ELIZA MARTIN (19 FEBRUARY 1902 SMITH COUNTY TX-06 MAY 1986 SMITH COUNTY TX)

Parents: William Monroe Martin and Mertie Alma Pool
     She is located in the 1930 census at Smith County, TX residing with a spouse and child.
     Mary married Lewis Henry Gus Dingler (28 July 1891 Smith County TX-23 June 1962 Smith County, TX) on 23 December 1922 in Smith County, Texas and was a schoolteacher. He was a farmer. They had one daughter, Martha L. (b. 1926 TX). (Moore, 2003)
     From the Social Security Death Index, it is discovered that Mary Eliza did not apply for a social security card until 1962. Both Mary Eliza and Lewis Dingler are listed in the LDS archives.

II.1.D.A.4.A (5) (A) 1 MARTHA L. DINGLER (B. 1926 TX)

Parents: Lewis Henry Gus Dingler and Mary Eliza Martin
     Martha married a gentleman with the surname Moore.

II.1.D.A.4.A (5) (B) SARAH E. MARTIN (B. 1905 TX)

Parents: William Monroe Martin and Mertie Alma Pool
     1920 census: Smith County, TX in the residence of her mother. Sarah was a registered nurse. (Moore)

II.1.D.A.4.A (5) (C) WILLIAM RAY MARTIN (B. 1907 TX)

Parents: William Monroe Martin and Mertie Alma Pool
     1920 census: Smith County, TX in the residence of his mother.
     1930 census: Smith County, TX and remained in his mother's house. Occupation was listed as laborer; single; middle name is Ray. Ray worked in shops and then as a railroad supervisor. (Moore)

II.1.D.A.4.A (5) (D) JEFF M. MARTIN (B. 1912 TX)

Parents: William Monroe Martin and Mertie Alma Pool
    1920 census: Smith County, TX in the residence of his mother.
    1930 census: Smith County, TX and remained in his mother's house.
    Jeff was manager of a five & dime store until World War II then was in ordinance in California during the war. He did various things after the war until he began working for General Dynamics in Ft. Worth, Texas in 1950. He retired from General Dynamics. (Moore)

II.1.D.A.4.A (5) (E) MARGARET F. MARTIN (B. 1915 TX)

Parents: William Monroe Martin and Mertie Alma Pool
    1920 census: Smith County, TX in residence of mother
    1930 census: Smith County, TX in residence of mother
    Margaret was with general hospital in France during WW II. She had joined the Red Cross intending to work with the organization for a year. She had her papers to be discharged when Pearl Harbor happened. She returned to Dallas and worked several years for a gynecologist then worked for Texas Instruments as an industrial nurse 1962 -1979. She had no children. (Moore)

II.1.D.A.4.A (6) NORA ELLA MARTIN (22 AUGUST 1875 AL-8 AUGUST 1960 LOS ANGELES, CA)

Parents: Zachariah Martin and Sarah L. "Pup" Stanley
    She married Ben F. Wilbanks (b. 1872 AL) 17 January 1897 in Smith County, TX. In the 1930 census the couple is located in Los Angeles, California owning their home at an estimated value of $5,000. Ben had no occupation listed, but Nora is annotated as a janitor. There are no children listed residing with them.

II.1.D.A.4.A (7) ANDREW ALFRED MARTIN (8 SEPTEMBER 1877 COVINGTON COUNTY, AL- 17 NOVEMBER 1962 SMITH COUNTY, TX)

Parents: Zachariah Martin and Sarah L. "Pup" Stanley

He was married twice. His first spouse was Lizzie Yarborough whom he married on 5 November 1899 in Smith County, TX. Her father provided a valuable commodity to Smith County during the Civil War.

The Civil War brought a flurry of activity to Smith County as the entire population was caught up in the excitement. The Confederate Government in 1863 purchased a private gun factory, begun by J. C. Short, William S. N. Biscoe, and George Yarborough to make rifles for the State of Texas. The gun factory expanded into the Confederate States Ordnance Works at Tyler, made around 2,233 rifles, repaired thousands of other weapons, produced millions of small arms and cannon cartridges, and employed around 200 men and boys. (Whisenhunt, 1983)

Andrew's second wife was Nellie Barron (27 August 1881 TX-July 1968 Smith County, TX) whom he married 20 June 1915 in Smith County.

Andrew had a total of four children from his combined marriages. Andrew and Lizzie had three children: Stephen M., Marcie M., and Edna E. Andrew and Nellie had one son Alfred M.

In the 1920 census, Andrew, Nellie and all the children resided in Smith County, TX. They were living five houses from his sister-in-law Mertie Pool Martin (see II.1.d.a.4.a {5}). His occupation was listed as a farmer.

In the 1930 census, he and Nellie, along with Alfred still were listed in the same residence. All the other children are gone by that time. They owned their home with an estimated value of $8,000. He is still listed as a farmer and the family has a servant, Henry Hawkins, residing with them.

Andrew is interred at Hopewell Cemetery in Smith County.

II.1.D.A.4.A (7) (A) STEPHEN MARION MARTIN (15 JANUARY 1901 TEXAS-02 SEPTEMBER 1982 SMITH COUNTY, TEXAS)

Parents: Andrew Alfred Martin and Lizzie Yarborough

1920 census: Smith County, Texas in residence of father and stepmother

II.1.d.a.4.a (7) (B) Marcie M. Martin (b. 1904 Texas)

Parents: Andrew Alfred Martin and Lizzie Yarborough
   1920 census: Smith County, Texas in residence of father and stepmother

II.1.d.a.4.a (7) (C) Edna E. Martin (b. 1908 Texas)

Parents: Andrew Alfred Martin and Lizzie Yarborough
   1920 census: Smith County, Texas in residence of father and stepmother

II.1.d.a.4.a (7) (D) Alfred M. Martin (b. 1918 Texas)

Parents: Andrew Alfred Martin and Nellie Barron
   1920 census: Smith County, Texas in residence of parents
   1930 census: Smith County, Texas in residence of parents

II.1.d.a.4.a (8) Nancy Eunis Martin (26 April 1879 AL-2 July 1962 Houston, TX)

Parents: Zachariah Martin and Sarah L. "Pup" Stanley
   She was the twin sister of Sarah Frances Martin and married John R. Franklin (1878 Texas-26 August 1945) on 9 June 1928 in Smith County, TX at the age of 48. They were farmers. She is interred in Hopewell Cemetery in Smith County.
   1930 census: Smith County, Texas

II.1.d.a.4.a (9) Sarah Frances Martin (26 April 1879 AL-14 July 1879 AL)

Parents: Zachariah Martin and Sarah L. "Pup" Stanley
   She died at the age of 2.5 months.

II.1.D.A.4.A (10) SHERMAN FIELDER MARTIN (7 APRIL 1885 AL-23 JANUARY 1926 HENDERSON COUNTY, TX)

Parents: Zachariah Martin and Sarah L. "Pup" Stanley

He was married twice: Eula Vertner Hayes in March 1907 and Essie Martin Luker on 5 March 1916. He and Essie had one son, Sherman Jr., and one daughter, Josephine. Sherman Sr. is interred at Rock Hill Cemetery in Henderson County, TX.

II.1.D.A.4.A (10) (A) SHERMAN FIELDER MARTIN, JR. (17 MARCH 1918 TX-26 JUNE 1992 SAN ANTONIO, TX)

Parents: Sherman Fielder Martin, Sr. and Essie Martin Luker

Following the death of his father, Sherman Jr. went to live with his aunt Nancy and her spouse, John Franklin. In the 1930 census, we find him in Smith County, Texas in the residence of the Franklins.

From his 1992 obituary, his spouse's given name was June and they had three sons: Douglas K., Scott F., and Randall B.

Major General Martin served in the United States Air Force for 30 years retiring in 1971. In WW II he flew 63 combat missions as a B-24 bomber pilot. After the war, he served as Deputy Commander of the Task Force for Operation IVY, a series of nuclear tests in the Pacific area, including the first hydrogen bomb test. He later became Chief, Atomic Operations Division, Directorate of Operations, J-3, in the organization of the Joint Chiefs of Staff. He also served as Chief of Staff, Plans for the Strategic Air Command; Commander in Chief, Strategic Air Command; Representative to the Joint Strategic Target Planning Staff and retired as Deputy Chief of Staff for Programs and Resources. His military decorations and awards included the Distinguished Service Medal, Legion of Merit, Distinguished Flying Cross with one oak leaf cluster, Air Medal with four oak leaf clusters, Purple Heart, and the Presidential Unit Citation Emblem with one oak leaf cluster.

Following retirement from the United States Air Force, he and his wife settled in San Antonio, TX where he was president of Randolph Men's Golf Association. (Obituary, *San Antonio Express-News,* Sunday, 28 June 1992)

II.1.D.A.4.A (10) (A) 1 DOUGLAS K. MARTIN

From his father's obituary in 1992, he had been MIA since the Vietnam War and his spouse, Karen L., was living in West Palm Beach, FL. His rank was that of captain.

II.1.d.a.4.a (10) (A) 2 Scott F. Martin

At the time of his father's death in 1992, Scott and his spouse were residing in Southlake, TX.

II.1.d.a.4.a (10) (A) 3 Randall B. Martin

At the time of his father's death in 1992, Randall and his spouse, Billie, resided in West Palm Beach, FL. They had one daughter, Heather M.

II.1.d.a.4.a (10) (B) Josephine Martin

Parents: Sherman Fielder Martin, Sr. and Essie Martin Luker

Josephine is listed in her brother's Sherman Jr. obituary in 1992 under her maiden name and resided in Oklahoma City, OK.

II.1.d.a.4.b. Henry "Hobbie" Martin (13 January 1849 Montgomery, AL-24 October 1906 Montgomery, AL)

Parents: Asbury Martin and Alice Hedgepath

He was placed with Simeon and Rebecca Hobbie following the death of his parents. Alice and Rebecca were intimate friends. The Simeon Hobbie family was childless at the time and reported to be quite wealthy. Upon adulthood, Henry changed his surname from Martin to Hobbie. Most of the records for his family are found under the Hobbie surname. He married Lenora Elizabeth Jackson (b. May 1852 AL) on 16 July 1872. They had seven children: Rebecca Alice (1874-1894 Montgomery, AL), John (b. 1875 Montgomery, AL), Richard (April 1878 Montgomery, AL-24 December 1940 Mobile, AL), Callie Elizabeth (b. 1879 Montgomery, AL), Henry Jr. (3 December 1880-23 February 1944 Montgomery, AL), Andrew Jackson (1 May 1884 Montgomery, AL-12 January 1959 Montgomery, AL), and Ame Lenora (5 June 1888 Montgomery, AL-23 November 1925 Asheville, NC).

1860 census: Montgomery, AL in the residence of Simeon and Rebecca Hobbie with annotated age as 11. The family is archived in the LDS library.

He left school in June 1868 and on January 1, 1869 entered the wholesale grocery establishment of LeGrand & Co. He was an employee for six years and a partner for four years. On January 1, 1879, together with W.F. Vandiver, he bought out LeGrand & Co. and the firm was named Hobbie & Vandiver, which continued until January 1883 when Hobbie sold out to Vandiver and formed a partnership with William M. Teague. (*Memorial Record of Alabama*, 1893, Volume 2, page 691)

Henry was co-owner of a wholesale grocery chain in Montgomery named Hobbie and Teague. The business is listed in the Montgomery City Directories for 1883-1895. In 1883 there was only one store at 533 South Court, but a second location was added in 1891 at 209-211 Commerce St. It is thought that his son, Henry Jr., took over operations sometime between 1920 and 1930.

II.1.D.A.4.B. (1) REBECCA ALICE MARTIN HOBBIE (1874-1894 MONTGOMERY, AL)

Parents: Henry "Hobbie" Martin and Lenora E. Jackson

II.1.D.A.4.B. (2) JOHN MARTIN HOBBIE (B. 1875 MONTGOMERY, AL)

Parents: Henry "Hobbie" Martin and Lenora E. Jackson

II.1.D.A.4.B. (3) RICHARD MARTIN HOBBIE (14 APRIL 1877 MONTGOMERY, AL-24 DECEMBER 1940 MOBILE, AL)

Parents: Henry "Hobbie" Martin and Lenora E. Jackson
   Spouse: Annie Henderson (d. December 1932 Tuscaloosa, AL)
   Children: Richard Jr., John, and Catherine
Richard acted as Conservation Chairman for Alabama during World War I. He was also a grocer in Montgomery.

II.1.D.A.4.B. (3) (A) RICHARD MARTIN HOBBIE, JR. (29 FEBRUARY 1908 MONTGOMERY, AL- 17 DECEMBER 1971 MONTGOMERY, AL)

Parents: Richard Martin Hobbie and Annie Henderson
   Spouse: Katherine Elizabeth Bush Hall
   Children: Helen Hall and Richard III

His obituary from December 1971 did not list any survivors. It did state that he died after a brief illness, was a member of the Trinity Presbyterian Church and was interred at Oakwood Annex Cemetery in Montgomery the day following his death. (Curd, 1990)

II.1.d.a.4.b. (3) (A) 1 Helen Hall Hobbie (17 January 1942 Montgomery, AL-02 November 1973 Jefferson County, AL)

Parents: Richard Martin Hobbie Jr. and Katherine Elizabeth Bush Hall
    Spouse: William Robert Calloway (09 August 1938 Autauga County, AL-02 May 1987 Autauga County, AL) Burial: Memory Garden
    Marriage date/place: August 1965 Montgomery, AL
    Children: Elizabeth Clare

II.1.d.a.4.b. (3) (A) 2 Richard Martin Hobbie III

Parents: Richard Martin Hobbie Jr. and Katherine Elizabeth Bush Hall
    Spouses: Margaret Davies and Anne Berridge
    He and Margaret had two children: Stephen Martin and Samantha Lynn.

II.1.d.a.4.b. (3) (A) 2.a Stephen Martin Hobbie

Parents: Richard Martin Hobbie III and Margaret Davies
    Spouse: Lindha Denise Schofield
    As of June 2003 they resided in Florence, AL.

II.1.d.a.4.b. (3) (A) 2.b Samantha Lynn Hobbie

Parents: Richard Martin Hobbie III and Margaret Davies
    Spouse: Kevin Douglas Schilf
    As of June 2003 they resided in North Carolina.

II.1.D.A.4.B. (3) (B) JOHN HOBBIE

Parents: Richard Martin Hobbie and Annie Henderson

II.1.D.A.4.B. (3) (C) CATHERINE HOBBIE

Parents: Richard Martin Hobbie and Annie Henderson

II.1.D.A.4.B. (4) CALLIE ELIZABETH MARTIN HOBBIE (B. 1879 MONTGOMERY, AL)

Parents: Henry "Hobbie" Martin and Lenora E. Jackson

II.1.D.A.4.B. (5) HENRY MARTIN HOBBIE JR (3 DECEMBER 1880 MONTGOMERY, AL- 23 FEBRUARY 1944 MONTGOMERY, AL)

Parents: Henry "Hobbie" Martin and Lenora E. Jackson

He married Bessie Shackelford Rogers (16 February 1887 Lowndes County, AL-September 1963 Montgomery, AL) on 18 January 1911 at Lowndes County, AL.

The family was located per the 1920 federal census in Montgomery, AL with one child, Henry M. Hobbie III. Henry Jr.'s occupation was listed as bank president. In the 1930 census, they remained in Montgomery and had another child, Ethel L. They owned their home with an estimated value of $16,000. Henry Jr.'s occupation had changed to proprietor of a wholesale grocery company, probably his father's chain.

Henry Jr. is listed in an edition of Who's Who in America as follows: *Encyclopedia of American Biography New Series*, vol. 18 and *Who Was Who in America. A component of Who's Who in American History*. vol. 3.

He was educated in public schools and Starke's University School in Montgomery and the University of Alabama at Tuscaloosa. He was a member of the Sigma Alpha Epsilon fraternity. In addition to taking over his father's grocery business, he also established the Hobbie Elevator Company, Hobbie Motor Company and Montgomery Buick Company. Mr. Hobbie was also President and a Director of the Fourth National Bank of Montgomery. His civic memberships included treasurer and member of the Executive Council, Boy Scouts of Montgomery; member of the Beauvoir Club and Montgomery Country Club. (*Alabama Blue Book and Social Register*)

II.1.D.A.4.B. (5) (A) HENRY MARTIN HOBBIE III (12 NOVEMBER 1911 MONTGOMERY, AL- 20 DECEMBER 1990 MONTGOMERY, AL)

Parents: Henry Martin Hobbie, Jr. and Bessie Shackelford Rogers
    Spouse: Henri-Lynn Street (10 February 1914-22 June 1998 Montgomery, AL)
    Marriage date: approximately 1934. Henri-Lynn's 1998 obituary stated, "She was preceded in death by her husband of 56 years." Children: Lynn Martin and Priscilla Street.
    1920 census: Montgomery, AL in residence of parents
    1930 census: Montgomery, AL in residence of parents
    March 1990: He is listed as a survivor in his sister Ethel's obituary residing in Montgomery, AL.
    His family called him "Bubba". (Davenport, 2003)
    Per his obituary in 1990, funeral services were held from the First United Methodist Church of Montgomery with internment in Oakwood Cemetery. Per her obituary in 1998, Henri-Lynn died in Birmingham. Her services also were held at the First United Methodist Church of Montgomery with burial in Oakwood Cemetery.

II.1.D.A.4.B. (5) (A) 1 LYNN MARTIN HOBBIE

Parents: Henry Martin Hobbie III and Henri-Lynn Street
    Spouse: Warren McCormick Andrews
    Children: Mary Elizabeth-Lee and Lynn Martin-Hobbie
    She was listed in her father's 1990 obituary as living in Birmingham, AL. Per her mother's 1998 obituary, she was annotated as living in Indian Springs Village, AL.
    Mary Elizabeth-Lee is listed in her grandfather's 1990 obituary under her maiden name. She is listed with surname as Lawley in her grandmother's 1998 obituary. Lynn Martin-Hobbie is listed under her maiden name in both her grandfather's and grandmother's obituaries.

II.1.D.A.4.B. (5) (A) 2 PRISCILLA STREET HOBBIE

Parents: Henry Martin Hobbie III and Henri-Lynn Street
    Spouse: Raymond Clyde Griffin, Jr.
    Priscilla is listed as living in Birmingham, AL in both her father's obituary (1990) and mother's obituary (1998). In neither obituary are any children mentioned.

II.1.D.A.4.B. (5) (B) ETHEL LEANN HOBBIE (3 MARCH 1920 MONTGOMERY AL-9 MARCH 1990 LAS VEGAS, NV)

Parents: Henry Martin Hobbie, Jr. and Bessie Shackelford Rogers

1930 census: Montgomery, AL in residence of parents

Ethel married Robert Milton Hope (8 February 1919 Sunny South, AL-22 August 1980 Palm Beach FL) in January 1941 in Montgomery, AL. They had two children: Nina Allison and Henry Martin.

Her obituary appeared in the *Las Vegas Review Journal* on 12 March 1990. Per the obituary, she had been a resident of Las Vegas for 10 years and had worked as a legal secretary. At the time of her death, she was survived by both children and her sibling, Henry Hobbie III. She had four grandchildren and two great-grandchildren. Private services were held. Ethel is interred at the Rogers Family Cemetery in Lowndes County, AL.

By the time of Robert's death in 1980, this couple was divorced. His obituary from the *Palm Beach Post* in 1980 lists Eleanor as his surviving spouse. Records reflect that his second spouse was Eleanor Durkee. His obituary also lists his son as Martin, who was living in Gresham, Oregon at the time, and daughter Nina, who was residing in Las Vegas. The obituary mentions that four grandchildren survived him, which is in keeping with research to date of Nina's three children and Martin's one daughter. We can conclude from the obituary that Martin's son was born after Robert's death in 1980. There was no visitation or funeral services for Robert, per his wishes, and the remains were cremated.

II.1.D.A.4.B. (5) (B) 1 NINA ALLISON HOPE

Parents: Robert Milton Hope and Ethel LeAnn Hobbie

Spouses: (1) Richard Ritzenthaler (31 May 1938 –15 August 1973 Madison, WI)

Children: Robert Thomas Phillips

Robert Thomas was living in Sauk City, Wisconsin at the time of his father's death.

Richard died from a self-inflicted gunshot wound. His obituary from the *Wisconsin State Journal* on 16 August 1973 mentions his son, Tom, but no other relatives except his mother and siblings. Per his obituary, Freeway Lumber Company and Ishnala Supper Club employed him.

Other spouses: (2) Robert Eugene Marshall Children: Hope Allison (3) Calvin Joe Davenport Children: Joanna Lynn (Davenport).

Nina was residing in Las Vegas, NV at the time of her father's death in 1980. His obituary lists her as Mrs. Joseph (Nina) Davenport. Her mother's obituary from 1990 lists Nina as still residing in Las Vegas.

II.1.D.A.4.B. (5) (B) 1 A ROBERT THOMAS PHILLIPS RITZENTHALER

Parents: Richard Ritzenthaler and Nina Allison Hope
   Spouses: (1) Deborah Ann Schroder Children: Brenda Loraine and Kevin Charles (2) Janet Lynn Hughes Children: Danielle Marie

II.1.D.A.4.B. (5) (B) 1 B HOPE ALLISON MARSHALL

Parents: Robert Eugene Marshall and Nina Allison Hope
   Spouse: Gene Paul Pasinski
   Children: Amanda Claire and Abigail Sophia

II.1.D.A.4.B. (5) (B) 1 C JOANNA LYNN DAVENPORT

Parents: Calvin Joe Davenport and Nina Allison Hope
   Spouse: Andrew Robert Carlson

II.1.D.A.4.B. (5) (B) 2 HENRY MARTIN HOPE, SR

Parents: Robert Milton Hope and Ethel LeAnn Hobbie
   Spouse: Jennifer Ann Hartman
   Children: Catherine Winslow and Henry Martin, Jr.
   He was residing in Gresham, OR at the time of his father's death in 1980. He was residing in Las Vegas, NV at the time of his mother's death in 1990.

II.1.D.A.4.B. (5) (B) 2 A CATHERINE WINSLOW HOPE

Parents: Henry Martin Hope, Sr and Jennifer Ann Hartman
   Spouses: (1) Michael Lee Nelson Children: Andrew James Nelson (2) Kevin Paul Bergan Children: none.

II.1.D.A.4.B. (5) (B) 2 B HENRY MARTIN HOPE, JR

Parents: Henry Martin Hope, Sr and Jennifer Ann Hartman

II.1.D.A.4.B. (6) ANDREW JACKSON MARTIN HOBBIE (1 MAY 1884 MONTGOMERY, AL- 12 JANUARY 1959 MONTGOMERY, AL)

Parents: Henry "Hobbie" Martin and Lenora E. Jackson

Andrew went by "Jackson". He married Minnie Lee Rainer (7 July 1889 AL-June 1980 AL) in 1910. The family is located in the 1930 federal census in Montgomery, AL. Three children are listed: Jackson, Minnie, and Elizabeth. Residing with them was a nephew, John W. Vardaman, age 14. They owned their home with an estimated value of $30,000 and Andrew is listed as president of a motor company. His career spanned time in both the wholesale grocery business and the automobile sales industry.

Jackson was educated in Starke's University School in Montgomery; St. Albans in Radford, Virginia; and Alabama Polytechnic Institute in Auburn, Alabama. His civic activities included deacon in the First Baptist Church of Montgomery, Mason, Shriner, and member of the Montgomery Country Club. His hobby was hunting. (*Alabama Blue Book and Social Register*)

Jackson's funeral service was held at the family's residence on Felder Avenue in Montgomery with internment following in Greenwood Cemetery. The family did include the nephew, John Vardaman, as a survivor in the obituary notice. There were no siblings listed as survivors. Per his granddaughter, "He was a fine man". (Davis, 2003)

II.1.D.A.4.B. (6) (A) JACKSON HOBBIE (30 MARCH 1913 MONTGOMERY, AL-11 JULY 1983 MONTGOMERY, AL)

Parents: Andrew Jackson Martin Hobbie and Minnie Lee Rainer
    1930 census: Montgomery, AL in residence of parents
    Spouse: Emily Whiting (divorced)
    Children: Emily, Virginia, and Mary
    He was interred in Greenwood Cemetery in Montgomery, AL.

II.1.D.A.4.B. (6) (A) 1 EMILY WHITING HOBBIE

Parents: Jackson Hobbie and Emily Whiting
    Spouse: Jacque Pebworth
    Per her father's 1983 obituary Emily was living in Montgomery, AL.
    Children: Mary Virginia, Rosemary, and Jacquelyn
    From Elizabeth Hobbie Davis September 2003 letter, Mary Virginia was married with the surname Wallace, Rosemary was married with the surname Key, and Jacquelyn was single.

II.1.D.A.4.B. (6) (A) 2 VIRGINIA WHITING HOBBIE

Parents: Jackson Hobbie and Emily Whiting
    Spouse: John Register
    Children: John Martin, Emily Hobbie, Paul Whiting, and Virginia Lynn
    Per her father's 1983 obituary, she was living in Montgomery, AL.

II.1.D.A.4.B. (6) (A) 3 MARY WHITING HOBBIE

Parents: Jackson Hobbie and Emily Whiting
    Spouse: Charles Blackwell (divorced)
    Children: none as of 2003
    Per her father's 1983 obituary, she was living in Millbrook, AL.

II.1.D.A.4.B. (6) (B) MINNIE HOBBIE (30 OCTOBER 1916 AL-APRIL 1996 MONTGOMERY, AL)

Parents: Andrew Jackson Martin Hobbie and Minnie Lee Rainer
    1930 census: Montgomery, AL in residence of parents
    Spouses: (1) Norvelle Lee Richardson (b. 1905) and (2) Raymond St. John
    Children: Minnie Lee Richardson
    Per her brother, Jackson's obituary in 1983, she was living in Montgomery, AL. By the time her sister, Elizabeth, died in 2000, she too was deceased as Elizabeth's obituary mentioned both her brother and sister preceded her in death.

II.1.D.A.4.B. (6) (B) 1 Minnie Lee Richardson

Parents: Norvelle Lee Richardson and Minnie Hobbie
   Spouse: Richard Hamilton Gill
   Children: Charles Nelson Gill
   She is listed in her Uncle Jackson's 1983 obituary as Minnie Lee Richardson Gill of Montgomery.

II.1.D.A.4.B. (6) (C) Elizabeth Hobbie (27 August 1919 AL-27 April 2000 Sumter, SC)

Parents: Andrew Jackson Martin Hobbie and Minnie Lee Rainer
   1930 census: Montgomery, AL in residence of parents
   Spouse: Joseph Edward Davis (1916-24 May 2003 Sumter, SC) Marriage date: 5 December 1942 Children: Elizabeth Hobbie and Joseph E.
   Elizabeth was a well-known dancing teacher who taught in Sumter, SC for 25 years. Per her obituary in *The Item* of Sumter, SC on 28 April 2000, she was a member of The Holy Comforter Episcopal Church where she taught Sunday School and was a member of the Episcopal Church Women. She was also a member of the Sumter Junior Welfare League, the Sumter Assembly Club, and the Sumter Cotillion Club where she helped with the debutantes for many years. She is interred in Evergreen Cemetery in Summerton, SC.
   Joseph was a native of South Carolina having been born in Summerton. He attended Summerton schools and graduated from the Citadel in 1938 with a degree in physics. He was a 1940 graduate of Georgia Tech with a degree in electrical engineering and of New York University in 1941 with a degree in meteorology.
   He entered the U.S. Army Air Corps in 1941 as a second lieutenant and received weather service training in 1941 at Gunter Field, AL. He attended flight school in 1942 at Orangeburg, Shaw, and Spence fields and then served as a pilot and weather officer during World War II (1943-1945) in the Aleutian Islands. He completed Air Corps Engineering School at Wright Field, Ohio, in 1946. He left active duty in 1947 at the rank of lieutenant colonel and served in the U.S. Air Force Reserve from 1947 to 1976, retiring with the rank of colonel.
   Upon settling in Sumter, he established Osteen-Davis Office Supply and Printing in 1947 and operated the business until selling it in 1985. He was a member of the Knock Rummy Group, the Road's End Club, the Millwood Club, the Thalian Club, the Sumter Cotillion, the Assembly Club, the American Legion, and the Air Force Association. He was a former member of the Cooper River Club, the Shelor Pond Club, the Sumter Lions Club, the Sumter Merchants Association-past president, and the Sumter Chamber of Commerce. He belonged to the Episcopal Church of the Holy Comforter, where he once served as a member of the vestry.

His funeral services were held at the Episcopal Church of the Holy Comforter with Rev. John M. Barr III and Rev. Mark R. Riggs officiating. Burial was in Summerton Evergreen Cemetery. Obituaries provided as courtesy of *The Item*, Sumter SC.

II.1.D.A.4.B. (6) (C) 1 Elizabeth Hobbie Davis (b. 28 June 1951)

Parents: Joseph Edward Davis and Elizabeth Hobbie

Spouse: Gregory Haywood Williams Marriage date: 16 December 1972 Children: Virginia Hobbie and Elizabeth Hobbie.

Per her uncle Jackson's 1983 obituary, she was living in San Antonio, TX. At the time of her mother's death in 2000, she was residing in Sumter, SC and remained there in 2003 per her father's obituary.

Virginia Hobbie Williams lived, at the time of her grandmother Elizabeth's death in 2000, in Austin, TX and was listed under her maiden name in the obituary. In 2003, she remained in Austin but had married as she was listed with a surname Bernal and a son, Joaquin Salvador, per her grandfather's obituary.

Elizabeth Hobbie Williams, at the time of her grandmother's death in 2000, was living in Austin, TX and listed under her maiden name in the obituary. As of 2003, per her grandfather's obituary, she remained single and was residing in Columbia, SC.

II.1.D.A.4.B. (6) (C) 2 Dr. Joseph Edward Davis, Jr. (b. 1 July 1949)

Parents: Joseph Edward Davis and Elizabeth Hobbie

Spouse: Ruth Roper Hutchinson. Marriage date: 25 July 1981. Children: Joseph Edward III and Ann Hughston.

Per his Uncle Jackson's 1983 obituary, he was living in Montgomery, AL. The obituary listed him with title of doctor. He remained in Montgomery per his mother's obituary in 2000 and father's obituary in 2003.

Joseph Edward Davis III was born 4 September 1983. Per his grandmother's (Elizabeth) obituary in 2000, he was living in Montgomery, AL. He remained there per his grandfather's obituary in 2003.

Ann Hughston Davis was born 2 April 1987. Per her grandmother's (Elizabeth) obituary in 2000, she was living in Montgomery, AL. She remained in Montgomery per her grandfather's obituary in 2003.

II.1.D.A.4.B. (7) AME LENORA "NONIE" MARTIN HOBBIE (5 JUNE 1888 MONTGOMERY, AL- 23 NOVEMBER 1925 ASHEVILLE, NC)

Parents: Henry "Hobbie" Martin and Lenora E. Jackson

She married John Wesley Vardaman (25 October 1880 Mt. Olive, AL-25 March 1927 AL) on 12 December 1912 in Montgomery. We find their son, John Jr., living with Andrew Jackson Martin Hobbie and Minnie Lee Rainer in the 1930 census at the age of 14 following the deaths of his parents.

II.1.D.A.4.B. (7) (A) JOHN WESLEY VARDAMAN, JR (22 JUNE 1915 MONTGOMERY, AL- 4 MAY 1979 CALHOUN COUNTY, AL)

Parents: John Wesley Vardaman, Sr. and Ame Lenora Martin Hobbie

1930 census: Residence of Andrew Jackson and Minnie Martin. Spouse: (1) Elizabeth Merrill (2) Derith Chase. Children: John W. Vardaman III "Jack" and Hugh Merrill Vardaman.

John Jr. was a prominent attorney in Anniston, AL with the firm of Merrill, Merrill and Vardaman. He attended Washington and Lee University from 1933-34. He received his bachelors' degree in 1936 and law degree in 1938 from the University of Alabama. He was admitted to the Alabama Bar Association in 1938.

He practiced law in Montgomery from 1938-39 and served as an assistant state attorney general from 1939-43. He served as director of, and attorney for, the Commercial National Bank of Anniston and a member at large of the Calhoun County Democratic Executive Committee. He was a member of Parker Memorial Baptist Church of Anniston. (Obituary 5 May 1979, *The Star*, Anniston, AL)

John Jr. is listed in: *Who's Who in America, 40ᵗʰ Edition* (1978), *Who's Who in American Law, 1ˢᵗ Edition* (1978) and *Who Was Who in America, Volume 7* (1981).

He is interred in Highland Cemetery in Anniston.

John "Jack" W. Vardaman III, per Jackson Hobbie's 1983 obituary, was listed as living in Washington, D.C. with spouse, Marianne. Two children were also mentioned: John Wesley IV and Davis.

Hugh is listed in the following biographical works: *Who's Who in American Law, 1ˢᵗ Edition, 1978 and Who's Who in American Law, 2ⁿᵈ Edition, 1979*. Per Jackson Hobbie's obituary in 1983, Hugh was living in Anniston, AL.

II.1.d.a.5 James Franklin Martin (24 March 1810 SC-5 November 1880 Clay County, AL)

Parents: John Martin, Jr. and Abigail Freeman

    1850 census: Clay County, AL

    For those Martin family members who came to Alabama from South Carolina and stayed but did not settle around Montgomery, we find five counties making up the bulk of their residency: Clay, Randolph, Calhoun, Talladega and Chambers. The history of this area is very similar, regardless of which county is the focus.

    Due to their location in a valley surrounded by mountains and plentiful water sources, settlers' main occupation in the beginning was agriculture. Of these relatives, many owned their farms and passed them on from generation to generation. The early settlers of this area were not owners of slaves and the farms were worked with white labor. Diversification of crops was the practice as well as a fruit culture and stock raising. Cotton was a predominant crop prior to the Civil War. There were several gristmills for grinding corn and wheat, cotton gins and sawmills, all using waterpower from the river and creeks to turn the mill wheels.

    After the Civil War, large mills were built and the economy quickly converted to textile manufacturing as the chief industry and major employer. This was especially true for the relatives settling around Chambers County. Manufacturing of "coarse fabrics" such as osanburg and single filling duck began there in 1866. Osanburg is a heavy, unbleached cotton cloth. It was used for goods such as farmers' clothing, overalls, sacking and bagging. Single filling duck was also a course fabric used for such things as tents, awnings, boat sails, tarpaulins and belts for machinery. (Owen, pp. 111-112)

    James married Margaret Walker (June 1810-December 1885) about 1830. In 2003 Henshaw writes, "James F Martin and his wife Margaret sold 218 acres of land located in Edgefield District, December 24, 1844 to Little Berry Freeman. This land was part of the estate of James Freeman, and was bought up in chars by James F. Martin. This land adjoined other land of James F. Martin. Before 1850 many families left Edgefield for the states of Georgia, Alabama, Florida and Mississippi. It was a movement that had widespread appeal and James F. Martin and his family joined the procession. They left Edgefield District sometime between 1850-1854, first settling in Cowetta Co., GA where a son Mitchell Chesley Martin was born in 1853. After three years they moved on to Talladega Co. AL where their daughter, Elizabeth Martin, was born in 1858."

    They had 11 children altogether and, except for the latter two, all were born in Edgefield County, SC. Those children were: Frances (17 September 1830-21 January 1911 Clay County, AL), Caroline (August 1832-20 March 1920 Clay County, AL), Chesley Burton (4 March 1834-3 September 1908 Calhoun County, AR), William Pheris (1837-27 March 1872 Clay County, AL), Martha (1839-1882 Clay County, AL), Henry Harrison (4 February 1841-7 February 1883 Clay County, AL), Samuel Bud (1843-1880 Clay County, AL), Sanders M. (10 March 1846-26 January 1916 Clay County, AL), James Allen (9 March 1848-2 July 1895 Calhoun County, AR),

Mitchell Chesley (10 August 1853-11 November 1897 Clay County, AL), and Elizabeth (15 April 1858-12 March 1943 Clay County, AL).

James F. Martin and family moved to Cowetta Co., GA, between 1850-1854, then to Talladega Co., AL, and on into Clay Co., AL. James Franklin Martin and Margaret Walker are buried in Olive Branch Baptist Church Cemetery, Lineville, Clay County, AL.

II.1.d.a.5.a. Frances Martin (17 September 1830-21 January 1911 Clay County, AL)

Parents: James Franklin Martin and Margaret Walker

She was married twice. Her first spouse was Newt Pearson (1830 GA-1863 AL) about 1856 in Georgia. They had three children: William Ransom (b. May 1857 Talladega, AL), Newton Edward (19 July 1861 Clay County, AL-15 December 1934 Chambers, AL), and Melissa (15 March 1860 Talladega, AL-25 March 1928 Clay County, AL).

Her second marriage was to Milton (some sources list him as Melton) Smith about 1866 and they had four children: James M. (12 February 1867 Clay County, AL-14 November 1945 Clay County), Charles H. (11 May 1869 Clay County, AL-23 January 1914 Clay County), Mary Margaret (February 1871-1949 Clay County, AL), and Allen H. (26 April 1872-22 June 1949 Clay County, AL).

1880 census: Milton and Frances with children in Clay County, AL. Occupation listed as farming.

II.1.d.a.5.a. (1) William Ransom Pearson (b. May 1857 Talladega, AL)

Parents: Newt Pearson and Frances Martin

His nickname was "Rance".

He married Eliza Elmira Devaughn (April 1861 AL-3 August 1935 Clay County, AL) on 23 December 1880 in Clay County, AL. Their children were: William Arthur, Cora, Lou Emma, Dixie E., Margaret Ethel, Newton Calvin, and Ezra. No additional data has been located for William Arthur, Cora, Margaret Ethel , and Newton Calvin.

Lou Emma married Marion J. Hulsey.

Dixie married Roy Burks and is found in the 1930 census residing in Clay County, AL in the Wesobulga Precinct with her spouse and a son, James R. Burks.

Ezra is found in the 1930 census living in the same Clay County precinct as Roy and Dixie Burks. He is annotated with a wife, Agnes, with year of marriage as 1922 and two children, Brit and Margrite. His occupation is listed as working for a power company. From the 1930 census, both Ezra's children were born in Alabama. The children's estimated years of birth from that data is 1922 for Brit and 1926 for Margrite.

Ezra's obituary appeared in the *Anniston Star* on 30 December 1981 page 7D. A maiden name for Agnes could not be confirmed. There were no surviving children listed, but three grandchildren and two great-grandchildren were mentioned although their names were not included. His services were conducted at Roanoke Church of Christ with burial in Randolph Memory Gardens.

II.1.d.A.5.A. (2) Newton Edward Pearson (19 July 1861 Clay County, AL-15 December 1934 Chambers, AL)

Parents: Newt Pearson and Frances Martin

He married Amanda "Mandy" Florella Wilson (9 September 1859 Randolph County, AL-16 November 1929 Chambers, AL) on 25 October 1883 in Clay County, AL.

In the 1920 federal census the family is located in Clay County, AL with the following children: May and Ola. Amanda's mother is also residing in the residence at the age of 84 and annotated as widowed. Newton's occupation is listed as farmer.

Other children born to this couple were Wyatt Buren, Margaret Emmie Beatrice, Avie Cornelia, Francis C., and Carrie Lavonia. (Grubaugh, 2003)

II.1.d.A.5.A. (2) (A) Wyatt Buren Pearson (4 September 1884-21 May 1962 Randolph County, AL)

Parents: Newton Edward Pearson and Amanda Florella Wilson

He married Earlie L. Lambert (30 July 1891 Clay County, AL-18 November 1953 Chambers, AL) on 3 November 1910 at Clay County, AL.

The family is located in the 1930 federal census in Randolph County, AL in the town of Fox Creek. Wyatt's occupation is listed as a saw mill operator. They have six children living with them: Newton D. (b. 1912 AL), Ernest (1914 AL-25 March 1989 Chambers County, AL), Theron (27 May 1915 AL-21 July 1998 Riverside, CA), George (b. 1918 AL), Addie P. (b. 23 December 1923 Clay County, AL), and Gladys (b. 1928 AL).

II.1.D.A.5.A. (2) (A) 1 Newton Donald Pearson (b. 1912 AL)

Parents: Wyatt Buren Pearson and Earlie L. Lambert

II.1.D.A.5.A. (2) (A) 2 Ernest Euvert Pearson (7 May 1913 AL-25 March 1989 Chambers County, AL)

Parents: Wyatt Buren Pearson and Earlie L. Lambert

Spouse: Clois Powell (1918 Marshall County, AL-5 March 1990 Valley, AL) Children: Edward

Euvert's obituary appeared in *The Valley Times-News* of Lanett, AL on 27 March 1989. Services were held at Johnson-Brown Service Funeral Home, Valley Chapel with Rev. Herbert Gray and Rev. Phil Davis officiating. Burial was in Rest Haven Cemetery. His spouse, son, two sisters, Addie Manley and Gladys Tillis, and one brother, Theron, survived him also with three grandchildren and two great-grandchildren. He was a native of Randolph County, AL and a member of New Harmony Congregational Church in Randolph County. He was a retired truck driver and veteran of World War II, serving with the U.S. Army in Italy.

Clois' obituary appeared in *The Valley Times-News* on 7 March 1990. Services were held at Johnson-Brown Service Funeral Home, Valley Chapel with Rev. Herbert Gray and Rev. Phil Davis officiating. Burial was in Rest Haven Cemetery. Her son; one brother, Roy Powell; one sister, Thelma Higgins; one niece, Maxine Bledsoe, and three grandchildren survived her. A native of Marshall County, AL she attended Shawmut Christian Church.

Edward was living in Houston, TX when his father died in 1989 and when his mother died in 1990.

II.1.D.A.5.A. (2) (A) 3 Theron Pearson (27 May 1915 AL-21 July 1998 Riverside, CA)

Parents: Wyatt Buren Pearson and Earlie L. Lambert

Theron is listed as a survivor in his brother Euvert's obituary in 1989, residing in California. His date and location of death were confirmed through Social Security Administration records.

II.1.d.a.5.a. (2) (A) 4 George Pearson (b. 1918 AL)

Parents: Wyatt Buren Pearson and Earlie L. Lambert

II.1.d.a.5.a. (2) (A) 5 Addie P. Pearson (b. 23 December 1923 Clay County, AL)

Parents: Wyatt Buren Pearson and Earlie L. Lambert

Addie was wed to Emory Gaines Manley (30 September 1917 Randolph County, AL-24 August 1987 Chambers County, AL) 10 March 1943 in Troup County, GA. Children: Joseph Harold.

Emory's obituary appeared in *The Valley Times-News* of Lanett, AL on 25 August 1987. The service was held at Johnson Brown-Service Chapel with Rev. Archie Gardner and Rev. Tommie Pritchett officiating. He was a native of Randolph County and attended Fairfax Congregational Holiness Church. A retired employee of Langdale Mill, he was a member of West Point Pepperell's 50-Year Club and a veteran of World War II, serving with the U.S. Army. Emory is interred in Fairfax Cemetery in Chambers County, AL. Addie was listed as a survivor in her husband's obituary in 1987 residing in Riverview, AL.

A separate article in the same edition of the newspaper highlighted his contribution to the community as well as his employment with West Point Pepperell: "He began working at the company's Langdale Mill on 1 June 1932 as a quill stripper in the weaving department. In October 1933, he transferred to the Prepatory (Twister) Department and worked there as a filling and warp doffer until 1942, when he left for service with the U.S. Army during World War II. He returned to the mill in September 1946 and continued as a filling and warp doffer until August 1971 when he moved to the Slasher Room. He worked there until his retirement on 1 August 1983. His father, two brothers, three sisters, wife and one son have worked for the company. His leisure interests included gardening, working with honey bees, fishing and reading."

Joseph Harold Manley was born 1 August 1947 in Chambers County, AL. In his father's obituary of August 1987, he is listed as residing in Fairfax, AL. He married Linda Shoemake on 27 Jun 1992.

II.1.d.a.5.a. (2) (A) 6 Gladys Pearson (b. 1928 AL)

Parents: Wyatt Buren Pearson and Earlie L. Lambert

March 1989: resided in Wadley, AL per her brother Euvert's obituary with surname as Tillis.

II.1.d.a.5.a. (2) (B) Margaret Emmie Beatrice Pearson (b. 29 April 1886 Randolph County, AL)

Parents: Newton Edward Pearson and Amanda Florella Wilson
 She married Bud Hamner.

II.1.d.a.5.a. (2) (C) Avie Cornelia Pearson (1 June 1887 Randolph County, AL– 10 May 1920 Randolph County, AL)

Parents: Newton Edward Pearson and Amanda Florella Wilson
 She married Milton Thurman Waldrop (12 January 1884 Randolph County, AL–13 June 1952 Orange County, FL) on 22 August 1907 at Randolph County, AL.

In the 1920 federal census the family is located in Randolph County, AL in the town of Fox Creek and Milton's occupation is listed as farmer. They have six children: Hoyt Lumas, Vida, Iverdale, Mae, Grace Lavonia, and Lue W. Following the 1920 census, Avie died and is buried in New Hope West Cemetery in Randolph County, AL.

Milton remarried following Avie's death to Julia Evelyn Caldwell Smith and the couple is found in the 1930 census in Coffee County, AL in the town of Deanville. By 1930, Hoyt and Viola have left the family to venture out on their own. A seventh child that had to belong to Milton and Avie, due to the estimated year of birth, is listed by the name of Virginia. Milton and Julia had nine children of their own, but since none of them would be related to the Barksdale lineage, their names have been omitted. Milton continued to farm while in Coffee County. Of interest is that all of the children who remained in the residence are annotated as farm laborers.

II.1.d.a.5.a. (2) (C) 1 Hoyt Lumas Waldrop (30 April 1908 Randolph County AL-22 September 1961)

Parents: Avie Cornelia Pearson and Milton Thurman Waldrop
 1920 census: Randolph County, AL in residence of parents
 Hoyt married Josie Cleone Fuller (29 November 1911 Elba, AL-22 February 1985 Fairfax, AL) on 30 July 1930 at Coffee County, AL. They had six children: Winford Porter, Ellen Cornelia, Tommy Gene, Kathryn, Raynell, and Hoyt Junior.

Hoyt died of a brain injury suffered in an auto accident. He and Josie are interred in Fairfax Cemetery in Chambers, AL.

II.1.d.A.5.a. (2) (C) 1 a Winford Porter Waldrop

Parents: Hoyt Lumas Waldrop and Josie Cleone Fuller
   He married Louise Huddleston of Troup County, GA. They had three children: Barry, Caroline, and Jo Ann.

II.1.d.A.5.a. (2) (C) 1 b Ellen Cornelia Waldrop

Parents: Hoyt Lumas Waldrop and Josie Cleone Fuller
   Spouse: Larry Dale Wimberly of Chambers County, AL. Children: Ronald Dale, Toni Nicole, Gerald Ray, and John Christopher.
   Ronald Dale married Sandra Wilson and they have a daughter, Tiffany Michelle. Toni Nicole married Steven Decker in Henry County, TN. No additional data exists for Gerald Ray and John Christopher.

II.1.d.A.5.a. (2) (C) 1 c Tommy Gene Waldrop

Parents: Hoyt Lumas Waldrop and Josie Cleone Fuller
   Tommy has a spouse, Beverly, and three children: Buzz, Collette, and Darren

II.1.d.A.5.a. (2) (C) 1 d Kathryn Waldrop

Parents: Hoyt Lumas Waldrop and Josie Cleone Fuller
   Spouses: (1) Parker Harris, (2) Donald Leak, (3) Mike Hill. Children: Patrick Leak and Ben Leak.

II.1.d.A.5.a. (2) (C) 1 e Raynell Waldrop (21 September 1934 Coffee County, AL-31 December 1992 Dougherty County, GA)

Parents: Hoyt Lumas Waldrop and Josie Cleone Fuller
   Raynell's first spouse was Jack Lamar Hughey (26 January 1926 Tallapoosa County, GA-3 June 1987 Elmore, AL). Their children were: Debra Lynn, David Lamar, Angelia Dianne, and Ronald Earl.

Debra Lynn has been married twice: Kerry Lewis Powell Boswell of Cowetta County, GA and David Philip Crosby. No data for children born of either marriage has been found.

David Lamar is married to Beverly Rae Shannon. They have two children: David Lee and Stephanie Lynn.

Angelia Dianne is married to Henry David Sullivan of Hendry, FL. They have two children: Kevin David and Brandie Diane. Kevin David Sullivan is married to Balinda Gail Graves of Henry County, TN and they have one son, Eric.

Ronald Earl is married to Shirley Jean Forthman of Hendry, FL. They have two daughters: Rhonda Jean and Jamie Paige. Rhonda Jean Hughey has had two spouses: (1) John McFarland Glover and (2) Robert Richard Decker.

Raynell's second spouse was Henry Lee Lashley. They had one son, Benjamin Lee. Benjamin Lee married (1) Patricia Ann Crull of Duval, FL and (2) Darlene Carswell of Albany, GA in 1982.

Her last spouse was Ernest Franklin Tyson (8 April 1929 Colquitt, GA-7 November 1991 Dougherty County, GA). There are no documented children for this couple.

II.1.D.A.5.A. (2) (C) 1 F Hoyt Junior Waldrop (7 August 1936 Chambers County, AL- 17 January 1979 Lincoln, Nebraska)

Parents: Hoyt Lumas Waldrop and Josie Cleone Fuller

Spouse: Judith May Fahrlander of Cass County, NE. Children: Tamara Marie, Jody Ann, and Marcy Dawn.

Tamara Marie married David Carlyle of Bellevue, NE. They have one child Karina Elizabeth born in Tulsa, OK.

Jody Ann married David Maurice Didano of Grand Prairie, TX. They have three children: Christine Marie, Benjamin Francis and Thomas Gregory, who were all born in Dallas, TX.

Marcy Dawn married David J. Lantz of Aurora, CO. They have one daughter, Vanessa Suzanne, born at York County, VA.

Hoyt Junior is interred in Fairfax Cemetery.

II.1.D.A.5.A. (2) (C) 2 Vida Beatrice Waldrop (18 May 1909 AL-26 May 1998 Russell County, AL)

Parents: Avie Cornelia Pearson and Milton Thurman Waldrop

1920 census: Randolph County, AL in residence of parents.

1965: Elba, AL per sister Grace's obituary (annotated as Rushing).

1988: Elba, AL per sister Louwade's obituary (annotated as Rushing).

Vida married Cecil Walter Rushing (20 January 1899 Coffee County, AL-20 November 1977 Coffee County, AL). Children: Maxine Miriam, Roland Darrell, Charlotte, Ronnie, and Opal Chastain.

Cecil's obituary appeared in the *Elba Clipper* on 24 November 1977. The Elba community knew him as "Peanut". His services were held on 21 November 1977 at the Haves Funeral Home Chapel with Rev. Milton Dykes and Rev. W.A. Thomas officiating. He is interred in Evergreen Cemetery. Survivors included his spouse, Vida; daughters: Chastine, Maxine and Charlotte; sons: Dairold and Ronnie; five sisters; two brothers; eight grandchildren and one great-grandchild.

II.1.D.A.5.A. (2) (C) 2 A MAXINE MIRIAM RUSHING (B. 1932 AL)

Parents: Cecil Walter Rushing and Vida Beatrice Waldrop
    1930 census: Phenix City, AL with spouse, Bennie Cole.
    1977: Phenix City, AL per father's obituary.
    As of 2003, this couple reside in Phenix City, AL.

II.1.D.A.5.A. (2) (C) 2 B ROLAND DARRELL RUSHING

Parents: Cecil Walter Rushing and Vida Beatrice Waldrop
    Spouse: Bettye Carter
    1977: Lakeland, FL per father's obituary.
    As of 2003, this couple lived in Inverness, FL.

II.1.D.A.5.A. (2) (C) 2 C CHARLOTTE RUSHING

Parents: Cecil Walter Rushing and Vida Beatrice Waldrop
    Spouse: Donald L. Latham
    1977: Mobile, AL per father's obituary

II.1.D.A.5.A. (2) (C) 2 D RONNIE RUSHING

Parents: Cecil Walter Rushing and Vida Beatrice Waldrop
    Spouse: Lisa Thompston
    1977: Albany, GA per father's obituary

II.1.d.a.5.a. (2) (C) 2 e Opal Chastain Rushing (3 November 1929-26 July 1993)

Parents: Cecil Walter Rushing and Vida Beatrice Waldrop
Spouse: Terrell McCord
1977: Dothan, AL per father's obituary

I.1.d.a.5.a. (2) (C) 3 Iverdale Buena Waldrop (27 March 1911 Randolph County, AL-? Chambers County, AL)

Parents: Avie Cornelia Pearson and Milton Thurman Waldrop
1920 census: Randolph County, AL in residence of parents
1930 census: Coffee County, AL in residence of father and stepmother
1965: River View, AL per sister Grace's obituary (annotated as Williams)
Iverdale was not listed as a survivor in her sister Louwade's obituary of October 1988.
Spouses: (1) Andrew Williams (2) Fred Allen Married at: Coffee County, AL
Children: Sybil Williams and Dorothy Williams

II.1.d.a.5.a. (2) (C) 4 Vera Mae Waldrop (7 October 1914 Randolph County, AL- 04 July 1942 Chambers County, AL)

Parents: Avie Cornelia Pearson and Milton Thurman Waldrop
1920 census: Randolph County, AL in residence of parents
1930 census: Coffee County, AL in residence of father and stepmother
Spouse: Roy E. Hadaway (17 November 1913-13 August 1990)
Children: Kenneth, Clinton, and Roland

II.1.d.a.5.a. (2) (C) 5 Grace Lavonia Waldrop (25 November 1915 Randolph County AL-9 December 1965 Chambers, AL)

Parents: Avie Cornelia Pearson and Milton Thurman Waldrop

1920 census: Randolph County, AL in residence of parents

1930 census: Coffee County, AL in residence of father and stepmother

Grace married Robert Judson Hussey on 22 September 1934 at Coffee County, AL. Children: Gwenell, Sandra, Janice, Jerry Marcus, and Charles.

Gwenell married William Beck. Sandra married Winfred Danford. Janice married Neal Miller. At the time of their mother's death, all lived in Fairfax, AL.

Jerry Marcus was born in Orange County, FL. He married Seidria Marlene Johnson of Chambers County, AL. They had two children: Randall Craig and Elizabeth Ann both of whom were born in Muskogee County, GA. Randall Craig Hussey married Joan Collier of Chambers County, AL. They have two children: Lacee McCall and Branden Collier. Elizabeth Ann Hussey married Kenneth Stanley Smith 1 August 1990 in Chambers County, AL. They have two children: Kenzlie Jordan and Railey Nicole.

No additional data exists for Charles other than that listed in his mother's December 1965 obituary.

Grace's obituary appeared in *The Valley Times-News* on 10 December 1965. She was struck by a "serious illness" three days prior to her death. She was a member of the Fairfax Congregational Holiness Church from which her services were held with Rev. Milton Bethune and Rev. Eugene Ziegle officiating. Burial was in Fairfax Cemetery. Survivors included her spouse of Fairfax; three daughters, Mrs. William Beck, Mrs. Winfred Danford and Mrs. Neal Miller all of Fairfax; two sons, Marcus Hussey of Fairfax and Charles Hussey of Greenville, SC; her stepmother, Mrs. M.T. Waldrop of Oakland, FL; three sisters, Mrs. Iva Williams of River View, Mrs. William Hollis of Fairfax and Mrs. Cecil Rushing of Elba. Six grandchildren also survived.

Her other siblings listed were those from her father's second marriage after her mother died. They were Mrs. Mildred Windham, Mrs. John Stine and Mrs. Richard Cyr all of Ocoee, FL, and Margaret Waldrop of Washington, DC. Three brothers also survived, Arnold and Clinton of Oakland, FL and J.D. of Winter Haven, FL.

II.1.d.a.5.a. (2) (C) 6 Louwade Haseltine Waldrop (25 September 1917 Randolph County, AL– 19 October 1988 Chambers County, AL)

Parents: Avie Cornelia Pearson and Milton Thurman Waldrop

1920 census: Randolph County, AL in residence of parents

1930 census: Coffee County, AL in residence of father and stepmother

1965: Fairfax, AL per sister Grace's obituary (annotated as Hollis)

She married William Hollis (26 March 1917-16 December 1978 Chambers County, AL). Children: James Marion and Linda.

Louwade's obituary appeared in *The Valley Times-News* on 19 October 1988. Graveside services were scheduled for 20 October 1988 at Fairfax Cemetery with Rev. Eugene Ziegle officiating. Survivors included son, James M. of Fairfax; daughter, Linda Yates of Fairfax; sister, Vida Rushing of Elba, AL and seven grandchildren. She was a homemaker and had been a resident of Valley, AL for 55 years.

II.1.D.A.5.A. (2) (C) 7 VIRGINIA FLORELLA WALDROP (9 JANUARY 1920 RANDOLPH COUNTY, AL- 23 AUGUST 1941 CHAMBERS COUNTY, AL)

Parents: Avie Cornelia Pearson and Milton Thurman Waldrop
    She married Howard Bassett (16 July 1922-30 August 2000 Chambers County, AL).

II.1.D.A.5.A. (2) (D) FRANCIS C. PEARSON (6 MARCH 1890 RANDOLPH COUNTY, AL- JANUARY 1974 RANDOLPH COUNTY, AL)

Parents: Newton Edward Pearson and Amanda Florella Wilson
    Spouse: Jake David Lashley (5 September 1889 Randolph County AL-1 June 1961 Randolph County, AL). Children: Mary Frances, Margaret, Charles Edward, Hulen Lavern, and Wilmer David. Two children died as infants.
    Mary Frances married Clifford Brown of Randolph County, AL.
    Margaret died on 3 October 1952 in Geneva County, AL. She had been a widow for some years prior to her death and had the surname Yarbrough.
    From Social Security Administration records, Charles Edward was born 22 November 1931 and died 21 August 1989 in Henry County, GA.
    Hulen Lavern was born 16 Jun 1916 and died in August 1958.
    No additional data exists for Wilmer David.

II.1.D.A.5.A. (2) (E) CARRIE ONNIE PEARSON (17 MAY 1892 RANDOLPH COUNTY, AL-9 SEPTEMBER 1964 RANDOLPH COUNTY, AL)

Parents: Newton Edward Pearson and Amanda Florella Wilson
    Spouse: George Walter Carson (22 December 1880-3 March 1960 Randolph County, AL).
Children: Edna, Elton, Durell, Ed, Cornelius, Fred, Harlice, Leon, and George Hugh.
    1930 census: Randolph County, AL

II.1.D.A.5.A. (2) (E) 1 Edna Lavonia Carson (B. 1924 Randolph County, AL)

Parents: George Walter Carson and Carrie Onnie Pearson
    1930 census: Randolph County, AL in residence of parents
    Spouse: Joe Harris
    Children: Joe Harris, Jr. and Ronald Harris
    Edna was listed, as a survivor in Elton's obituary in 1998 and living in Anniston, AL.

II.1.D.A.5.A. (2) (E) 2 Elton Carson (4 November 1912 Randolph County, AL-9 April 1998 Lee County, AL)

Parents: George Walter Carson and Carrie Onnie Pearson
    1930 census: Randolph County, AL in residence of parents
    Spouse: Marie Atkins (22 June 1921 Randolph County, AL-6 March 1999 Lee County, AL). Children: Bradford and Sheila.
    From Elton's 1998 obituary, Bradford was married to a female with the first name Dora and they lived in Opelika, AL. Sheila resided in Atlanta, GA upon Elton's death with her maiden name listed in the obituary.
    Elton's obituary appeared in the Lee County newspaper. From that data we learn that he was a lifetime member of Fairfax United Methodist Church and a member of the Valley Masonic Lodge. He was an avid gardener and gospel singer for most of his life and was a retired employee of West Point Pepperell's Fairfax mill. His internment is in Forrester's Chapel Cemetery near Wadley, AL.

II.1.D.A.5.A. (2) (E) 3 Durell Carson (14 April 1917 Randolph County, AL – 2 August 1994 Russell County, AL)

Parents: George Walter Carson and Carrie Onnie Pearson
    1930 census: Randolph County, AL in parents' residence
    Spouse: LaMerle Kitchens (23 March 1919-9 September 2002 Russell County, AL) Children: Linda.
    He is not listed as a survivor in Elton's obituary of 1998.

II.1.D.A.5.A. (2) (E) 4 ED CARSON (1913 RANDOLPH COUNTY, AL-15 DECEMBER 1998)

Parents: George Walter Carson and Carrie Onnie Pearson
    Spouse: Ethel Gray
    Children: Mike, Steve, and Gwen
    Gwen married Marvin C. Barton (Crosby, March 2003).
    Ed is not listed as a survivor in Elton's obituary of 1998.

II.1.D.A.5.A. (2) (E) 5 CORNELIUS CARSON (1 JUNE 1920 RANDOLPH COUNTY, AL-27 SEPTEMBER 2001)

Parents: George Walter Carson and Carrie Onnie Pearson
    1930 census: Randolph County, AL in residence of parents
    Spouse: Louise Cosper
    Children: Neda, Darrell, Barry, Marsha, Janice, and Sharon

II.1.D.A.5.A. (2) (E) 6 FRED N. CARSON (B. 1929 RANDOLPH COUNTY, AL)

Parents: George Walter Carson and Carrie Onnie Pearson
    1930 census: Randolph County, AL in residence of parents
    Spouse: Mary Walker
    Children: none found
    Fred is listed as living in Ashland, AL in Elton's obituary of 1998.

II.1.D.A.5.A. (2) (E) 7 HARLICE CARSON (B. 1922)

Parents: George Walter Carson and Carrie Onnie Pearson
    1930 census: Randolph County, AL in parents' residence
    Spouse: Mary Alice Ferguson (b. 14 January 1926 Tallasee, AL) Children: Beverly (Carson, 2003)
    Harlice is listed in his brother's obituary of 1998 as living in Phenix City, AL.

II.1.D.A.5.A. (2) (E) 8 Leon Carson (circa 1915)

Parents: George Walter Carson and Carrie Onnie Pearson
Leon died as an infant.

II.1.D.A.5.A. (2) (E) 9 George Hugh Carson (2 February 1931 Randolph County, AL-4 March 1951 Randolph County, AL)

Parents: George Walter Carson and Carrie Onnie Pearson
There is no 1930 census listing for George Hugh, which would indicate he was born after that time. According to his brother Harlice (2003), "George was never married."
George is not listed as a survivor in Elton's obituary from 1998.

II.1.D.A.5.A. (2) (F) Liza Eddie May Pearson (31 December 1897 Randolph County, AL-11 December 1989 Chambers County, AL)

Parents: Newton Edward Pearson and Amanda Florella Wilson
1920 census: Clay County, AL in residence of parents
Liza was never married.
Her obituary appeared in *The Valley Times-News* of Lanett, AL on 12 December 1989. Her services were held at Fairfax Congregational Church on 13 December 1989 with Rev. Ronald Cook and Rev. David Parker officiating. Burial was in Fairfax Cemetery. Her only survivor was a sister, Ora, of Fairfax. She was a native of Randolph County, AL, and a member of New Hope Missionary Baptist Church in Cragford, AL. She was a retired employee of West Point Pepperell's Fairfax Mill where she was a weaver.

II.1.D.A.5.A. (2) (G) Ora Lavonia Pearson (3 August 1898 Clay County, AL-23 January 1992 Chambers County, AL)

Parents: Newton Edward Pearson and Amanda Florella Wilson
1920 census: Clay County, AL in residence of parents
Ora was never married.

Her obituary appeared in *The Valley Times-News* of Lanett, AL on 24 January 1992. Funeral services were scheduled for 26 January 1992 at Fairfax Holiness Church with the Rev. Ronnie Cook and Rev. David Parker officiating. Burial was in Fairfax Cemetery. Nieces and nephews of whom none were listed by name survived her. A native of Clay County, AL, she was a member of New Hope Baptist Church and attended Fairfax Holiness Church. She was a retired employee of West Point Pepperell's Fairfax Mill.

II.1.D.A.5.A. (3) MELISSA PEARSON (15 MARCH 1860 TALLADEGA, AL-25 MARCH 1928 CLAY COUNTY, AL)

Parents: Newt Pearson and Frances Martin

She married George R. Denham (9 December 1855 GA-9 November 1924 Clay County, AL) on 12 July 1882 in Clay County, AL.

The family is located in the 1900 federal census in Clay County, AL. There were seven children listed in the residence: James H., Robert R., Joseph F., Elizabeth, Fannie M., Wyatt Edward, and an unnamed daughter (believed to be Ida who is listed in 1920). George's occupation in all censuses is listed as farmer.

They remain in Clay County at the 1920 census. Elizabeth, Wyatt Edward and Ida remain in the residence. Also included is their daughter, Fannie Giles, who is annotated as widowed with her children, Edna L. and William D.

One child, Nuten Abner, died prior to any census listings for this family.

Both George and Melissa are deceased in the 1920s.

II.1.D.A.5.A. (3) (A) JAMES HENRY DENHAM (AUGUST 1885 CLAY COUNTY, AL-DECEMBER 1953)

Parents: Melissa Pearson and George R. Denham

1900 census: Clay County, AL in residence of parents

1920 census: Winter Garden, FL

He married Alice Adoline Willis (7 October 1890 Clay County, AL-16 July 1931 Winter Garden, FL) on 20 January 1907 at Clay County, AL.

They had five children: Lessie Pearl, Luther, Ocis, Oren, and Vida B. All are listed in the 1920 census. No additional data has been found for Luther, Ocis, and Vida.

Lessie Pearl Denham was born 16 December 1907 in Clay County, AL and died 26 April 1948 in Florida. She was not married.

Oren Denham was born 12 November 1916 in Alabama and died January 1967 in Newton County, MS (Social Security Administration records).

II.1.d.a.5.a. (3) (B) Robert Ransom Denham (6 July 1887 AL-21 August 1979 Alachua, FL)

Parents: Melissa Pearson and George R. Denham
   1900 census: Clay County, AL in residence of parents
   1920 census: Clay County, AL in own residence with wife, no children
   1930 census: Orange County, FL; he and wife, no children
   His spouse was Georgianna Augusta (01 June 1885 AL-20 January 1970 Marion, FL) whom he married in 1909.
   In the 1920 census his occupation is listed as tenant farmer and in 1930 as poultry man.

II.1.d.a.5.a. (3) (C) Joseph Franklin Denham (b. June 1891 AL)

Parents: Melissa Pearson and George R. Denham
   1900 census: Clay County, AL in residence of parents

II.1.d.a.5.a. (3) (D) Elizabeth Denham (b. July 1893)

Parents: Melissa Pearson and George R. Denham
   1900 census: Clay County, AL in residence of parents
   1920 census: Clay County, AL in residence of parents

II.1.d.a.5.a. (3) (E) Fannie M. Denham (b. February 1895 AL)

Parents: Melissa Pearson and George R. Denham
   1900 census: Clay County, AL in residence of parents.
   1920 census: Clay County, AL in residence of parents annotated under married name of Giles and listed as widowed.
   Fannie married Claud Bryan Giles and he died before 1920 when he was only 25. They had two children, Edna L. and William D., who are listed in the 1920 census in the residence of their Denham grandparents.

II.1.d.a.5.a. (3) (F) Wyatt Edward Denham (17 August 1898 Clay County, AL- January 1976 Winter Haven, FL)

Parents: Melissa Pearson and George R. Denham
    1900 census: Clay County, AL in residence of parents
    1920 census: Clay County, AL in residence of parents

II.1.d.a.5.a. (3) (G) Ida Denham (b. April 1900 AL)

Parents: Melissa Pearson and George R. Denham
    1900 census: Clay County, AL in residence of parents and annotated as unnamed daughter
    1920 census: Clay County, AL in residence of parents

II.1.d.a.5.a. (3) (H) Nuten Abner Denham (3 October 1883 Clay County, AL-22 September 1894 Clay County, AL)

Parents: Melissa Pearson and George R. Denham

II.1.d.a.5.a. (4) James M. Smith (12 February 1867 Clay County, AL-14 November 1945 Clay County)

Parents: Milton Smith and Frances Martin
    He married Annie B. May (13 December 1873 AL-03 December 1960 Clay County, AL) 11 October 1891 in Clay County, AL.
    The family is located in the 1920 federal census in Clay County, AL in the town of Ashland. Living in the residence of James and Annie are four children: George B., John Wesley, Lula O., and Eulie. In 1930, they remained in Clay County with John Wesley and Eulie still in the residence. James' occupation is that of farmer.

II.1.d.a.5.a. (4) (A) George B. Smith (24 September 1902 Clay County, AL-9 December 1946 Tallapoosa County, AL)

Parents: James M. Smith and Annie B. May
    1920 census: Clay County, AL in the residence of parents

II.1.d.a.5.a. (4) (B) John Wesley Smith (b. 1912 AL)

Parents: James M. Smith and Annie B. May
    1920 census: Clay County, AL in the residence of parents
    1930 census: Clay County, AL in the residence of parents
Annotated as Wesley in the 1920 census and John W. in the 1930 census.

II.1.d.a.5.a. (4) (C) Eulie Smith (b. 1915 AL)

Parents: James M. Smith and Annie B. May
    1920 census: Clay County, AL in the residence of parents
    1930 census: Clay County, AL in the residence of parents

II.1.d.a.5.a. (4) (D) Lula O. Smith (b. 1905 Clay County, AL)

Parents: James M. Smith and Annie B. May
    1920 census: Clay County, AL in the residence of parents

II.1.d.a.5.a. (4) (E) Lee J. Smith (b. August 1896 Clay County, AL)

Parents: James M. Smith and Annie B. May
    This child does not appear in any of the censuses in which his parents are found. Debra Crosby supplied his name.
    1930 census: Clay County, AL

He married Lillie B. (6 June 1899 AL-8 August 1990 Clay County, AL) in 1924. Her dates of birth and death are confirmed from Social Security Administration records.

Children listed in the 1930 census: Jamie M., Oles F., and Will__ L.

II.1.d.a.5.a. (5) Charles H. Smith (11 May 1869 Clay County, AL-23 January 1914 Clay County)

Parents: Milton Smith and Frances Martin

He married Lee Ola (1 May 1880 AL-14 February 1931 Clay County, AL).

Children: Ida, Marcus M., Russell T., and unnamed infant

No additional data has been located for Ida.

Marcus married Annie Lizzie (5 January 1898 AL – 4 December 1966 Clay County, AL).

Russell married Louise Suggs (25 March 1910 AL – 5 December 1959 Clay County, AL).

Infant Smith was born 18 December 1908 and died 3 January 1909 in Clay County, AL. The grave is in the Smith Cemetery in Clay County, AL.

II.1.d.a.5.a. (6) Mary Margaret Smith (February 1871 Clay County, AL-1949 Clay County, AL)

Parents: Milton Smith and Frances Martin

She married Martin Luther Powell (23 May 1863 AL-February 1924 Clay County, AL) on 25 December 1890 in Clay County, AL. Justice of Peace S.N. Griffin performed the marriage.

The family is located in the 1920 federal census as residing in Clay County, AL in the town of Wicker. Three children are annotated: Nellie B., Mittice, and Abner B. Mary is listed as Margerette in this census.

No additional data has been located on Nellie. Other researchers have listed Mittice's spouse as Curtis Wheelis and Abner's spouse as Louise Johnson. However, corroborating evidence is lacking.

An obituary for Abner was located, but the information is scant. The only confirmable information from the obituary is that his date of birth was 13 May 1909 and that he died in October 1987 in Clay County, AL.

Margaret was located in the 1930 census residing in the residence of Sanders Smith in Clay County, AL in the town of Wicker. Sanders is Margaret's nephew through her brother, Allen. She is annotated as Margerett in 1930.

II.1.d.a.5.a. (7) Allen H. Smith (26 April 1872-22 June 1949 Clay County, AL)

Parents: Milton Smith and Frances Martin

He married Della A. Gamel (15 August 1875-08 November 1933) on 17 December 1891 in Clay County, AL. Justice of Peace John W. Miller performed their marriage.

The only census record of this family is in 1930 where they resided in Clay County, AL in the town of Ashland and owned their farm. Five children are listed in the residence at this census: Luther L., Allen Brazel, Ava Belle, C.B., and Hugo.

Researcher, Robert Smith, has documented five additional children for this couple who most likely had left the family residence by the 1930 census. Their names were Curtis L., Sanders, Ross, Darthula, and Chester V.

No additional data has been located for Luther, Ava, or C.B.

Smith has Allen listed as marrying Louise Jones. His Social Security Administration records have his date of birth as 04 October 1910 and his date of death as 31 October 1972.

Hugo's Social Security Administration records show his date of birth as 02 December 1918 and his date of death as 01 June 1966.

Curtis' obituary gave his date of birth as 12 April 1894 and his date of death 20 May 1929 in Clay County, AL. Beyond that, no additional information has been located.

Smith has Sanders listed as marrying Ruby L. Walker (b. 1898 AL). Per the data from the 1930 census, the year of marriage is estimated as 1914, assuming this was a first marriage for both of them. The family is located in the 1930 federal census in Clay County, AL in the town of Wicker. They have one daughter, Inez. He is annotated as A. Sanders and his occupation is listed as farmer. From that same census, one can estimate the year of Inez's birth as 1922.

Smith has Ross listed as marrying Mary Riddle and has Darthula listed as marrying Sam Williams.

Additional data on Chester V. Smith is gleaned from his Social Security Administration records. In those, his date of birth is listed as 03 September 1907 and his date of death is 14 January 1977.

II.1.d.a.5.b Caroline Martin (August 1832 SC-20 March 1920 Clay County, AL)

Parents: James Franklin Martin and Margaret Walker

She married John Jackson Allen (December 1822 GA-1907 Clay County, AL) on 17 August 1852 in Cowetta County, GA. He and Caroline were very much in love, and when he heard her family was moving to Georgia, he immediately went to the Martin home and arranged to move with them. He and Caroline married some time later and settled in Clay County, AL.

They had eight children. Unless otherwise noted all the children were born, married and died in Clay County, Alabama. They were James P. (12 March 1855-16 April 1894), Margaret (January 1857-?), John Henry (b. January 1858), Chesley Burton (March 1862-4 April 1931), Lucinda (22 February 1867-5 January 1941 Callahan, TX), William Timothy (19 February 1869-12 July 1950), George Columbus (1871-1937), and Ezelle "Eliza" (b. 1876).

Caroline is annotated in the 1920 census in Clay County, AL residing in the residence of her son, William Timothy, at the age of 87 and widowed. The date of enumeration was 22 January, so it is assumed that, when she died in March 1920, she resided there still.

II.1.D.A.5.B. (1) JAMES P. ALLEN (12 MARCH 1855 CLAY COUNTY, AL-16 APRIL 1894 CLAY COUNTY, AL)

Parents: John Jackson Allen and Caroline Martin

He married Louisa "Luiza" Moon (4 December 1861-18 November 1936 Clay County, AL) on 4 December 1879 in Clay County, AL. They had six children: Vernie Ann, Young John, James Hiram, Martin Luther, Elizabeth, and Dora, who died as an infant.

The 1880 census has James listed in Clay County, AL.

The only other census records found pertaining to this family are listed under Louisa as the head of the household. She appears in the both the 1920 and 1930 census in Clay County, AL. In 1930, she is listed as owning the residence with an estimated value of $2000. Her son, Young, is listed as residing in the residence.

II.1.D.A.5.B. (1) (A) VERNIE ANN ALLEN (B. DEC 1880)

Parents: James P. Allen and Louisa Moon

II.1.D.A.5.B. (1) (B) YOUNG JOHN ALLEN (18 OCTOBER 1884 CLAY COUNTY, AL-22 OCTOBER 1963 CLAY COUNTY, AL)

Parents: James P. Allen and Louisa Moon

1930 census: Clay County, AL in residence of his mother where he is annotated as a general store merchant. He was unmarried.

II.1.d.a.5.b. (1) (C) James Hiram Allen, Sr (4 October 1886 Clay County, AL-8 March 1958 Clay County, AL)

Parents: James P. Allen and Louisa Moon

He is found in both the 1920 and 1930 censuses living in Clay County, AL with spouse, Ivy Mae Giles (23 October 1890 AL-10 May 1986 Clay County, AL), and three children: James Hiram, Jr., Louise, and Mary L.

James Sr. was the Clay County Sheriff per the 1930 census.

James, Jr., was born 8 July 1913 and died 4 October 1991 per his Social Security Administration records. No additional information has been located for his sisters.

II.1.d.a.5.b. (1) (D) Martin Luther Allen (8 November 1889 Clay County, AL-23 June 1936 Clay County, AL)

Parents: James P. Allen and Louisa Moon

Martin Luther and Rita Kathleen Gibson (26 March 1893 AL-September 1983 Clay County, AL) were wed in 1917. They had two children: James L. "Jim" and Martin Luther "M.L." In the 1930 census, Martin's occupation is listed as a merchant, general store. The family owned their home with an estimated value of $2500.

Jim married Louise Harr on 29 November 1941 in Clay County, AL. Louise had migrated to Alabama from Oregon where she was born in Copper on 23 November 1920. They had a daughter named Dixalee "Dee Dee." Louise died in Medford, OR on 26 September 1987 and Jim in 1998.

Dee Dee married John Edgar Norton on 29 December 1962 at Chanute Air Force Base, IL. There are no documented children.

Beyond the information in the 1930 census, there is no additional information on Martin and Rita's other son, Martin, Jr. From that census, his year of birth is estimated as 1925.

II.1.d.a.5.b. (1) (E) Elizabeth Allen (1888 Clay County, AL-June 1890 Clay County, AL)

Parents: James P. Allen and Louisa Moon

Elizabeth is interred in the Baptist Church cemetery in Ashland, AL with her tombstone engraved as "Little Lizzie".

II.1.d.A.5.b. (1) (F) Dora Allen (1882-April 1890 Clay County, AL)

Parents: James P. Allen and Louisa Moon

Dora is interred in the Baptist Church cemetery in Ashland, AL.

II.1.d.A.5.b. (2) Margaret Allen (b. January 1857 Clay County, AL)

Parents: John Jackson Allen and Caroline Martin

She married James Sterling Ray about 1875. Their children were: Carrie, Thadeus, Major A., Richard C., Marshall, Ossie V., Abbie B., Lillie, Annie B., Irena, and Vasti.

The only census record of this family is from 1920. In that year, Margaret is listed in Clay County, AL, living in Ashland. She had one daughter, Vasti, living in her residence. James had died prior to the 1920 census as Margaret is annotated as widowed.

From the 1920 census data, Carrie's year of birth is estimated as 1876 and Thadeus' birth year as 1878. No other information has been found for them.

In the 1930 census, Major is located in Coosa County, AL as a farmer. From this census, his year of birth is estimated at 1882. He has a spouse named Johnnie and two children: Claude A. and Daniel M. Again, from the census, Major and Johnnie's year of marriage is estimated at 1902. We find in Claude's Social Security Administration records his date of birth was 11 April 1908 and his date of death as 19 August 1993 in Macomb County, MI. No additional data was located on Daniel, but one can estimate from the 1930 census that his year of birth was 1919.

The only other child born of James and Margaret for whom information has been found is Marshall. He was born in March 1883 and died during December 1924 in Choctaw County, AL per his tombstone. His spouse was Myrtle. They had a daughter Ruby Lea. All three are buried together at a rural cemetery in Choctaw County, AL after dying as the result of a house fire.

II.1.d.A.5.b. (3) John Henry Allen (January 1858 Clay County, AL-19 July 1887 Clay County, AL)

Parents: John Jackson Allen and Caroline Martin

He married Sarah Ann Beasley Wood (b. August 1859 GA) on 19 July 1877. Judge of Probate James L. Williams performed their marriage at Clay County, AL. Children: Olive D., Estella, Blanch Rook, Pascal Jackson, John Erma, and Doris O.

Of their children, the only one of whom additional information has been located is Pascal. From his Social Security Administration records, he was born 21 November 1882 in Clay County, AL and died in January 1971 at Plainview, TX.

II.1.D.A.5.B. (4) CHESLEY BURTON ALLEN (MARCH 1862-4 APRIL 1931)

Parents: John Jackson Allen and Caroline Martin

He married Thurza M. Ray (1862 AL-?) on 25 October 1884.

The family is located in Clay County, AL in the town of Ashland in both the 1920 and 1930 federal census. In 1920, there are three daughters in the residence: Rosalie E., Sybil P., and Grace E. The only daughter remaining in 1930 is Rosalie. Chesley's occupation in 1920 is annotated as president of the First National Bank and, in 1930, president of Ashland Railroad.

From information received by correspondence, the couple had nine children: Cleveland W., Rosalie Ezelle, Marvin Columbus, Eric Chesley, Sybil P., Eustace A., Ruth V., Mary Claud, and Grace E.

Rosalie was born October 1886 in Clay County, AL from information in the 1930 census. She died 09 October 1953 at Clay County, AL. She was never married.

In the 1930 census, Sybil is found living in Coosa County, AL with spouse, O.B. Farrell, and no children. From that census, their year of matrimony is estimated to be 1925. Mr. Farrell's occupation was listed as an automobile dealer.

In her brother Eustace's obituary in December 1968, Sybil is annotated as living in Douglasville, GA. Sybil's obituary appeared in the *Douglas County Sentinel* 6 July 1988. Her survivors included only nieces and nephews. She is interred in Highland Cemetery in Anniston, AL. From her obituary, she was born 30 July 1892 in Clay County, AL and died at Douglasville, GA on 1 July 1988.

From the 1920 census, Grace's year of birth is estimated to be 1902. No additional information has been found on Grace. However, in Eustace's 1968 obituary, he is listed as survived by two sisters. It has already been determined Sybil was Mrs. Farrell. Since the remainder of his sisters had predeceased him by 1968, one presumes that Grace was the other sister, listed as Mrs. H.S. Horton and living in Carrollton, GA in 1968.

While Cleveland does not appear in any of the census data with his parents, his existence is known from the estate documents of Eustace Allen, his brother. Going back into the census data, Cleveland is found in 1920 at Clay County, AL with estimated year of birth as 1885. He had a spouse with the first name Edith. In 1930, Cleveland, Edith and three children lived in Volusia County, FL. Cleveland's occupation in both census listings is attorney.

His children were Cleveland Jr., Edith M., and Jeane. No additional information is available for the children, although Cleveland Jr. was listed as a survivor in his Aunt Sybil's 1988 obituary.

Since Cleveland is not listed in Eustace's 1968 obituary, one presumes he was deceased prior to 1968.

Marvin Columbus was born in 1889 in Clay County, AL and died in 1891 in the same.

Eric Chesley was born October 1890 in Clay County, AL and died 14 November 1941 at Jefferson County, AL. His spouse was Eula Hooten. She remained in Alabama following Eric's death where she died in 1961 at Clay County. There are no documented children for this couple.

Eustace was a neurosurgeon in Atlanta, GA. He was born 3 October 1894. In the 1920 census, he is enrolled in the residency program of Mercy Hospital at Baltimore, MD. He died on 7 December 1968 in Fulton County, GA. In Eustace's obituary from *The Atlanta Constitution* on 9 December 1968, his survivors include a spouse (no name listed) and two sisters, Mrs. H.S. Horton of Carrollton, GA and Mrs. O.B. Farrell of Douglasville, GA. His internment was in Ashland, AL. Pallbearers were members of the Fulton County Medical Society. There were no children listed as survivors in his obituary.

Ruth was born 15 September 1897. She died March 1986 in Townshend, VT. In Ruth's obituary from 1986, the only information on her spouse is his last name of Evans, that he preceded her in death and they were married for 45 years. The only survivors listed were nieces and nephews.

Finally, Mary Claud was born 19 August 1899 in Clay County, AL and died 14 February 1900 at the same. Evidence of her existence is in the estate papers of Eustace.

II.1.D.A.5.B. (5) LUCINDA ALLEN (22 FEBRUARY 1867-5 JANUARY 1941 CALLAHAN, TX)

Parents: John Jackson Allen and Caroline Martin

She married William Elison Pruett. H.M. Evans, Justice of the Peace, performed their marriage on 26 October 1884 in Clay County, AL.

II.1.D.A.5.B. (6) WILLIAM TIMOTHY ALLEN (19 FEBRUARY 1869 CLAY COUNTY, AL-12 JULY 1950 CLAY COUNTY, AL)

Parents: John Jackson Allen and Caroline Martin

He was married twice. His second spouse was Susie E. Cronin (1 July 1885 AL-15 July 1968 Bullock County, AL) whom he married in 1923 as estimated from the 1930 census. His first spouse and mother of his children was Cora M. Horn (22 February 1886 -13 May 1919 Clay County, AL) whom he married on 23 August 1896.

William Timothy is found in the 1920 census in Clay County, AL in the town of Ashland. In that year, he is annotated as widowed. There are seven children, plus his mother, residing in the residence. The children are Hubert, Alta, Mabel, Carlton, Carrie Lee, Annie, and Joseph M. William's listed occupation is farmer.

In the 1930 census, William remained in Clay County and is annotated with wife, Susie, and children, Annie and Joseph. He continued to farm.

In the 1920 census, Susie Cronin is found in Dallas County, AL as a matron at the Alabama Methodist Orphanage.

Little information has been found on the children of William Timothy. In some researchers' notes, Mabel is spelled Maybell. Two researchers have an eighth child listed for William – James - with an estimated birth year as 1908. A possible reason for no census listing would be that James died prior to the 1920 census.

II.1.D.A.5.B. (7) GEORGE COLUMBUS ALLEN (1871 CLAY COUNTY, AL-1937 CLAY COUNTY, AL)

Parents: John Jackson Allen and Caroline Martin

He married Mary Browning (1875 AL-25 December 1943 Etowah County, AL) in 1899.

In the 1920 federal census, the family is found residing in Etowah County, AL in the town of Gadsden. George's occupation is listed as attorney. There are three children annotated: George Jr., James, and William J. Additionally, Mary's sister, Mildred C. Browning, is listed as well as four roomers.

In the 1930 census, the family remained in Etowah County with all the children in the household.

George Columbus served in the Alabama State Senate and was known as Judge Allen. His son, James, became an United States Senator representing the state of Alabama.

II.1.D.A.5.B. (7) (A) GEORGE COLUMBUS ALLEN JR. (1910 AL-18 AUGUST 1958 ETOWAH COUNTY, AL)

Parents: George Columbus Allen and Mary Browning

1920 census: Etowah County, AL in the residence of his parents

1930 census: Etowah County, AL in the residence of his parents where he is listed as divorced and an accountant at a rubber plant.

Per his obituary on 20 August 1958 from *The Gadsden Times*, his only survivors were his two brothers. "Mr. Allen was a native and life-long resident of Etowah County. He was a graduate of Gadsden High School and a construction worker. He was a veteran of World War II, having served in the Seabees."

George is interred in Forrest Cemetery in Gadsden, AL.

II.1.D.A.5.B. (7) (B) Senator James Browning Allen (28 December 1912 Etowah County, AL-1 June 1978 Baldwin County, AL)

Parents: George Columbus Allen and Mary Browning
  1920 census: Etowah County, AL in the residence of his parents
  1930 census: Etowah County, AL in the residence of his parents

> *Common sense in an uncommon degree is what the world calls wisdom. This tribute was written beside his picture in the Gadsden High School annual of 1928, the year he graduated as valedictorian at the age of 15. His classmates never had reason to change their minds. (The Gadsden Times, 03 June 1978)*

He was twice married, first to Margie Stephens, who died when their home burned. He married Maryon Pittman Mullins in 1964 at Birmingham, AL. The two met when James was lieutenant governor of Alabama and, as a newspaper reporter, she interviewed him. She survived him.

Children: James B. Allen, Jr. and Maryon Allen. At the time of the Senator's death, James Jr. was residing in Tuscaloosa, AL and Maryon, listed by her married name as Walker, was living in Tuscaloosa.

He began his law practice, with his father, in Gadsden in 1936. James was elected to the Alabama House of Representatives in 1938. Re-elected to the House in 1942, he resigned his seat to serve in the Navy during WW II from 1943 to 1946. He was a member of the Alabama Senate from 1946 to 1950. He was Lieutenant Governor of the State of Alabama from 1951 to 1955 and again from 1963 to 1967. He was first elected to the United States Senate in 1968, re-elected in 1974 and continued to serve until his death, June 1 1978.

The *Opelika-Auburn News* of Alabama carried an eight-column spread: *Sen. Allen's Powerful Voice Silenced.* He died of an apparent heart attack at the age of 65. Senator Edward Kennedy, among those, who praised Senator Allen, made the statement that Allen was "perhaps the greatest parliamentarian ever to sit in the United States Senate." North Carolina Democratic Senator Sam Ervin said, "We really can't afford to lose Jim Allen. He had intelligence, he had industry and he had the courage to stand up for what he knew to be right."

According to the newspaper account, his most celebrated stand came against the two Panama Canal treaties approved by the Senate on March 16 and April 18 1978. (Woodson, H. 1980)

His funeral was held at the First United Methodist Church of Gadsden, AL with Sen. Ervin, Sen. Harry F. Byrd, Jr. of Virginia, and Dr. O.B. Sansbury, pastor of the church as eulogists. Then Vice-President Walter Mondale and First Lady Rosalynn Carter headed the delegation from the executive branch of the federal government to pay tribute to Senator Allen. He is interred in Forrest Cemetery in Gadsden, AL.

His spouse, Maryon, was appointed to her husband's vacant Senate seat on 6 June 1978. However, she lost her bid for election in the Democratic Primary later that same year. In the years since Senator Allen's death, she has been a columnist for The Washington Post, public relations and advertising director for C.G. Sloan & Company and an entrepreneur, starting her own restoration and design company.

II.1.d.a.5.b. (7) (c) William J. Allen
(1911 AL-1993 Miami, FL)

Parents: George Columbus Allen and Mary Browning
    1920 census: Etowah County, AL in the residence of his parents
    1930 census: Etowah County, AL in the residence of his parents
    At the time of his brother's death in 1978, William was residing in Miami, FL.
    His obituary appeared in the *Miami Herald* on 26 February 1993 and was very brief. No survivors were listed and private services were held with Philbrick and Lithgow Coral Gables Chapel handling arrangements.

II.1.d.a.5.b. (8) Ezelle "Eliza" Allen
(b. 1876 Clay County, AL)

Parents: John Jackson Allen and Caroline Martin
    She married Joseph D. Mitchell (b. 1866 Kentucky) on 15 August 1894 in Clay County, AL. In the 1930 census, they lived in Callahan, TX. Joseph's occupation was listed as a proprietor of a blacksmith business. They owned their home with a value of $3,000. Children: Erma D. and Audrey M.
    Erma was never married. From her Social Security Administration records, her date of birth was 5 August 1917 in Texas and her date of death as 18 October 1996 at Los Angeles, CA.
    In 1930, Audrey and her spouse, Noah Cook, were living in the residence of her parents. From that census, their estimated year of marriage is 1927. Noah's occupation was listed as an electrician apprentice. From Social Security Administration records, Audrey's date of birth was 23 October 1902 in Texas and she died at Gaines County, TX in January 1985. Like her sister Erma, Audrey and Noah must have migrated further west at some point as Noah's death is listed as August 1982 in Santa Barbara, CA.
    Barksdale descendants migrated from Alabama and South Carolina into Arkansas. Specifically, the area chosen was the southern central area known as Calhoun County.
    The area had been primarily occupied by Choctaw Indians up until the early 1800's. The first pioneers began settling here in 1841. A group of settlers from Chambers County, AL formed a small community later known as Chambersville. Two of the earliest pioneers, W. S. Thornton and

Asa R. Cone, arrived by following the old "Checo Trace", an overland route from the Mississippi River across southern Arkansas, which involved them cutting a path to bring their wagons through to the make the first settlement. By 1846, this community in Moro Township had its first store and a post office, both owned and operated by Dr Bass. (Calhoun County ArGenWeb Project)

Settlers began to first come to the region due to access by water transportation on the Ouachita River and the rich sandy loam soil. Acres of available land that was easily cultivated drew immigrants from Alabama, Tennessee and Georgia. The county was made up primarily of farming families with cotton being the main cash crop. Many owned land for the first time as they took advantage of the Homestead Act to buy public land.

Originally, these areas were part of Dallas County. Settlers had to travel to the county seat to conduct civil business, purchase land, and obtain licenses and bonds as required by law. Dallas and Ouachita Counties, at the time, both were extensive in size, leaving the residents in the eastern portions of their counties having to travel long distances to conduct these affairs. With this in mind, an Ouachita County Representative, Thomas Woodward, agreed to divide Ouachita County and have the General Assembly form a new county for the convenience of its citizens.

Calhoun County, Arkansas was formed on December 6, 1850 by the Arkansas General Assembly who carved it from portions of Dallas, Ouachita and Bradley Counties to give the area citizens a more centrally located seat of government. The county was named for John C. Calhoun, an early Vice President of the United States, serving under John Quincy Adams and Andrew Jackson. The county is approximately 36 miles in length and 24 miles in width encompassing about 610 square miles. (Calhoun County ArGenWeb Project)

Merchants bought their stock at New Orleans and had it shipped up the Ouachita River to Little Bay Landing, 12 miles south of Hampton. The numerous landings along the river enabled steamboats to unload the goods brought from New Orleans and receive the cotton and other products for the return trip. Calhoun County became a busy center of activity.

Then, as it did to all parts of the south, Civil War came. Calhoun County's Civil War heritage was the 400 plus men it sent into battle. It should be noted about 40 men from the county enlisted in the Union Army. Although no military engagements occurred in the county, the halt of cotton trade suspended all business. Many of the merchants closed down shop to enlist. By the end of the war there wasn't a single business left. As a footnote, the immigration the county enjoyed before the war ended as well. It would not be until the 1880's and the appearance of a railroad it began again with settlers mainly coming from Alabama. (Calhoun County ArGenWeb Project)

In 1883, the St. Louis, Arkansas and Texas Railway laid tracks in southern Arkansas and the northwest corner of the county. It was later absorbed by the Cotton Belt Railway. The immense natural resource of forests of southern yellow pine timber now could be harvested and brought to market. Tracks were laid through Caswell Township and a railroad and saw mill town grew up overnight. The two saw mills in Thornton, one in Little Bay and one at Eureka Station, employed well over 300 men and their payrolls supported a prosperous county heading into the 20th century. The capacity in 1890 of the mills was near 36 million board feet annually. As of the 2000 census, the population was 5,744, ranking Calhoun County as the smallest in Arkansas by population. (Calhoun County ArGenWeb Project)

II.1.d.a.5.c CHESLEY BURTON MARTIN (4 MARCH 1834 EDGEFIELD COUNTY, SC-3 SEPTEMBER 1908 CALHOUN COUNTY, AR)

Parents: James Franklin Martin and Margaret Walker

He married Martha Adeline Ware (23 October 1839 Talladega, AL-7 April 1911 Calhoun County, AR) on 2 November 1854 in Talladega. S.E. Swope performed their marriage. They moved from Alabama to Arkansas about 1858.

Chesley Burton served Confederate States of America Company B, 1st Arkansas Calvary, from 3 Mar 1862 to May 1865.

Chesley and Martha were granted 80 acres on 3 June 1882 under the Homestead Treaty of 20 May 1862 in the township of Camden of the state of Arkansas and are considered to be among the first Arkansas landowners. Chesley B. Martin had a "bottom-land" homestead of 160 acres (perhaps added to) which he used to raise cotton. The tax records of 1862 show the Martins owned a slave valued at $600.

The family is found in the following federal censuses residing in Calhoun County, AR: 1860, 1870, 1880, and 1900. They were of the Methodist faith.

They had 10 children – unless otherwise noted all dates of birth, marriage and death occurred in Calhoun County, Arkansas. Those children were: Thomas Henry (28 February 1859 Talladega, AL-July 1882), Ruth H. (23 September 1859-5 August 1897 Dallas County, AR), Martha (19 November 1862-13 October 1865), James Edwin (20 August 1866-12 December 1937 Bradley County, AR), Georgia Etta (25 November 1868-22 September 1876), Lula Lenora (1 January 1871-11 April 1931), Allen Burton (8 July 1873-27 October 1942 Pine Bluff, AR), William Elbert (14 July 1875-9 November 1943), Alice Ware (28 April 1878-12 April 1962 Houston, TX), and Robert Chesley (14 July 1882-1961 Pine Bluff, AR).

Both Chesley Burton Martin and Martha Ware Martin are interred in Ricks Cemetery in Calhoun County, AR.

II.1.d.a.5.c (1) THOMAS HENRY MARTIN (28 FEBRUARY 1859 TALLADEGA, AL-JULY 1882)

Parents: Chesley Burton Martin and Martha Adeline Ware

He never married and remained on the family farm until his death in 1882.

II.1.d.a.5.c (2) Ruth H. Martin (23 September 1859-5 August 1897 Dallas County, AR)

Parents: Chesley Burton Martin and Martha Adeline Ware

She married Sterling V. Wood (8 June 1847 MS-21 June 1917 Calhoun County, AR) in 1886 at Calhoun County, AR. Sterling owned 40 acres in Camden, AR that he purchased on 04 August 1880.

They had two children: Myrtle and Parnam. From census data, Myrtle was born 10 February 1889 and Parnam was born 29 August 1891.

Sterling and Ruth are both interred in Ricks Cemetery in Calhoun County.

II.1.d.a.5.c (3) James Edwin Martin (20 August 1866-12 December 1937 Bradley County, AR)

Parents: Chesley Burton Martin and Martha Adeline Ware

He is found in the 1920 census as living in Bradley County, AR with a spouse and four children. In the 1930 census, he remained in the same location with the same spouse, one of the children from the 1920 census and an additional child.

He married Bell Zora Higgason (b. November 1868 AR) about 1896. They had five children: Madarosa B, Mary E., Carlton, Ruth, and John T.

On 08 April 1903, James was granted 160 acres in Sumpter, AR in accordance with the 1862 Homestead Treaty. In 1920 and 1930, the couple was annotated as owning their farm.

Madarosa is reported to have married a gentleman with the surname Rowland. Her estimated birth, from the 1930 census, is November 1896 in Bradley County, AR.

Mary remained in the residence of her parents through 1930. Her estimated year of birth is 1899. No further data has been located on Mary.

In 1920, Carlton's occupation is listed as a farm laborer – believed to be on the farm owned by his family. He married Sallie Childs in approximately 1920 from the ages at first marriage annotated in the 1930 census. In 1930, Carlton lived in the town of Clay, Arkansas with wife, Sallie C. (b. 1902 AR), and the following four children: Edward C. (b. 1921 AR), Vickie S. (b. 1924 AR), Sara F. (b. 1926 AR), and Jean (b. 1928 AR). Sallie's father, William Childs, also resided in their residence. Carlton continued to farm and they are annotated as owning their farm in 1930.

No additional information beyond the 1920 census has been located for Ruth. From that census, her year of birth is estimated to be in 1904.

In the 1930 census, John is annotated as divorced and working on his parents' farm. From that census, his year of birth is estimated at 1907. No explanation has been found as to why he did not appear in the 1920 census listing with his family. A separate census listing for him in 1920 has not been located.

II.1.D.A.5.C (4) LULA LENORA MARTIN (1 JANUARY 1871-11 APRIL 1931)

Parents: Chesley Burton Martin and Martha Adeline Ware

She married Julian Rockett Abernathy (9 October 1866 Calhoun County, AR-14 April 1919 Calhoun County, AR) on 30 October 1890 at Calhoun County. They had 12 children (all born in Harrell, AR): Hosea B., Jessie Lee, Julian Ray, Otis Ware, Irene, Boyd Martin, Gertrude, Edna, Mary, Mamie, Jackson Dean, and Adeline. Adeline was born and died on 15 November 1915.

In the 1920 census, we find Lula located in Calhoun County, AR with all of her children in the residence except Hosea, Jessie Lee and Irene. Also annotated is a daughter-in-law, Pearl, who is assumed to have been Julian Ray's spouse as he is the only child annotated as married in the census. Both Julian Ray and Boyd are listed as farm laborers.

In the 1930 census, Lula remained in Calhoun County, continuing to own the farm that she and Julian established. Living with her was son, Dean, and daughter, Mamie.

Julian Rockett Abernathy is interred in Ricks Cemetery at Calhoun County.

II.1.D.A.5.C (4) (A) HOSEA B. ABERNATHY (25 OCTOBER 1891 CALHOUN COUNTY, AR-10 JANUARY 1983 SPRINGHILL, LA)

Parents: Julian Rockett Abernathy and Lula Lenora Martin

Hosea was drafted for WWI from Calhoun County, AR. He married Margaret Patton (b. 10 September 1892 AR) approximately 1918 (year estimated from information contained in 1930 federal census). The family is located in the 1930 census in Richland County, OH in the town of Madison. They have one daughter, Louise.

Hosea's obituary appeared in the Springhill, LA newspaper. He was a resident of Fountain View Nursing Home and died following a long illness. A native of Harrell, AR, and a resident of Springhill for 45 years, he was a retired carpenter with 43 years of civil service. His services were held at Bailey Mortuary Chapel on 11 January 1983 with Rev. Jerry Phillips officiating. Burial was in Welcome Cemetery. Survivors included his daughter, Louise; five sisters, Mamie, Gertrude, Edna, Mary and Otis; two grandchildren, Charles Walker and Mary Gregory.

Louise Abernathy died two years after Hosea (25 March 1921 AR-September 1985 Baxter County, AR). She married Brent Courtright Walker on 29 June 1939. They had four children: Billy Sene, Bobby Wayne, Charles, and Mary.

Billy Sene Walker (10 January 1942-21 April 1967) died in Vietnam. Bobby Wayne Walker (11 January 1944-5 August 1944) died as an infant.

Charles Walker was resided in Lexington, KY and Mary Walker lived in Houston, TX at the time of their grandfather, Hosea's, death in 1983. Mary was listed in the obituary with the surname Gregory.

II.1.d.a.5.c (4) (B) Jessie Lee Abernathy (9 February 1893 Calhoun County, AR- 18 August 1976 Bradley County, AR)

Parents: Julian Rockett Abernathy and Lula Lenora Martin

He is found in the 1920 census residing in Calhoun County, AR with a wife and one child. In 1930, he is located in Bradley County, AR with a wife and two children.

Jessie married Olivian Burnett (29 December 1898 AR-6 August 1985 AR) on 29 November 1917. In 1920, they were living next to his mother and other siblings. By 1930, they had moved to Bradley County, town of Warren, where they rented their home for $25 month. Jessie's occupation is listed as traveling salesman in the 1930 census. In both the 1920 and 1930 censuses, his name is spelled Jesse. Jessie and Olivian had two sons: Charles Lathan and Ned Vernon.

From the 1930 census, Charles' birth date is estimated as December 1919. Charles married a woman with the surname La Frances. They had two daughters. One daughter married a Kerst and the other daughter married a Hillard. Both daughters had two children as well.

Ned Vernon Abernathy (27 August 1923 AR-March 1986 Union County, AR) married Anne Collins on 30 April 1943. Anne's death of date is 25 September 1976 in Tyro, AR. They had two children: a son and a daughter. No information is available on the son, but the daughter married a Bowman and had two children.

II.1.d.a.5.c (4) (C) Julian Ray Abernathy (2 September 1894 Calhoun County, AR- 17 December 1967 Union County, AR)

Parents: Julian Rockett Abernathy and Lula Lenora Martin

As previously stated, Julian was living in the residence of his mother in the 1920 census with a spouse, Pearl. While no other census information reveals anything new about Julian Ray, research completed by other genealogists gives some basic facts. He married Jennie Pearl Searcy Fisher (25 July 1894 Poss, AR-December 1986) on 20 December 1919. The location of that marriage has been annotated both as Calhoun County and Little Rock, AR, depending on which source one references. Most researchers agree they had two children: Julian Ray, Jr. and Peggy Lou. Both Julian Ray Sr. and Jennie Pearl are interred in Campground Cemetery in Calhoun County.

Other genealogists annotate Julian Ray, Jr. as marrying Juanita F. Angels (25 October 1918-16 March 2000 Bexar County, TX) on 25 July 1941. They had three children, two males and one female. A search of the *San Antonio Express-News* 16-23 March 2000 for an obituary on Juanita proved fruitless.

Other genealogists have annotated Peggy Lou's marriage to Dion Gammil (9 September 1927 AR-10 May 1993 Longview, TX) occurring on 6 June 1951. They had three children: Gay, Jennifer and Michael.

Dion's obituary appeared in the *Longview News-Journal* on 13 May 1993.

> *Graveside services for Dion L. Gammil, 65, of Longview will be 2 p.m. Friday at Camp Ground Cemetery in Hampton, AK under direction of Rader Funeral Home of Longview. He was born September 9, 1927 in Stephens AK. He was a retired truck driver for a local oil company. Survivors include wife, Peggy; daughters, Gay Peppers and Jennifer Cannon, both of Longview; son Michael of Colorado Springs, CO; six grandchildren and a number of nieces and nephews.*

Follow-up has discovered the newspaper used the wrong state abbreviation in the obituary for Arkansas. Dion was never in Alaska; he lived in Arkansas throughout his life.

II.1.d.A.5.c (4) (D) Otis Ware Abernathy (13 February 1896 Calhoun County, AR- 13 July 1987 Bradley County, AR)

Parents: Julian Rockett Abernathy and Lula Lenora Martin

She married Prather G. Temple (15 September 1900 Bradley County, AR-24 December 1944 Little Rock, AR) on 22 October 1921 in Bradley County, AR. They had three children: Francis, Norwood and Lawrence.

1920 census: Calhoun County, AR in the residence of her mother

1930 census: Bradley County, AR with spouse, two children and both in-laws

1983 residence: Warren, AR, per brother Hosea's obituary

Most of what has been discovered about this family began with a review of Prather's and Otis' obituaries. Otis' obituary is as follows:

> *Mrs. Otis Abernathy Temple, age 91, of Route 2, Box 503-A, Warren, died Monday, July 13 (1987), at the Bradley County Memorial Hospital. She was the widow of Prather G. Temple who died December 24, 1944. Mrs. Temple was born February 13, 1896 at Harrell, a daughter of the late Julian R. Abernathy and Lula Martin Abernathy. She was a homemaker and a Methodist. Surviving are 2 sons, Norwood Temple, Warren and*

Lawrence Temple, Haunville, LA; 1 daughter, Francis Carter, Kenner, LA; 4 sisters, Mamie Timms, Stamps AR, Edna Bays, Corpus Christi TX, Gertrude Ivy, LaMarque TX and Mary Ruth Funk, Duncan MS; 7 grandchildren and 13 great-grandchildren. Funeral services were 2:00 p.m. Wednesday July 15 at Frazier's Chapel of the Chimes by Rev Row Williams. Mrs. Phyllis Williams was in charge of the music. Burial was in the Ebenezer Cemetery by Frazier's Funeral Home. Pallbearers were Mack Williams, Ronald Wilson, Raymond Greenwood, A.W. Walker, Edwin Sanders, Roger Gorman, Jack Phillips and Van Mayo. (Altman, 2003)

Prather's obituary is as follows:

News of the sudden death of Prather G. (Goule) Temple in a Little Rock Hospital came as a surprise to his many friends in Bradley County this week. Mr. Temple was actively engaged as a blacksmith and welder, operating his shop on South Myrtle St., until he entered the hospital a short time ago. He was born in Bradley County on September 15, 1900, and died on Dec. 24, 1944. He was a member of the Masonic Lodge and also belonged to the Baptist Church. He is survived by his wife, Mrs. Otis Temple, one daughter, Mrs. Frank Carter; two sons, Norwood and Lawrence Temple, all of Warren; one brother, E.D. Temple; two sisters, Mrs. Jewell Wear and Mrs. Nora Hairston; two half brothers, Jesse and Cleveland Ferguson also of Warren. The Rev. Paul Aiken held funeral services at the Ebenezer Baptist Church on Tuesday afternoon, Dec. 26. Pallbearers were R.G. Garrison, Keith Sanders, Warner Neely, Edward Lyon, Glynn Lyon and Morgan Munford. (Woodard, 2003)

Francis Temple married James Ross Carter who died 9 March 1983. From her mother's obituary, in July 1987 she lived in Kenner, LA. A subsequent search of the Social Security Index does not turn up any records for her. The couple had two children (Thomason, 2003).

Norwood Temple (17 September 1926 AR-29 December 1989 Bradley County, AR) married a woman with the surname Sanders and they had four children. At the request of the family, names have been omitted. (Thomason, 2003)

Lawrence Temple is not listed with the family in the 1930 census which has caused many researchers to omit him completely from their notes. However, he existed according to the obituaries of both of his parents. He also is listed as a pallbearer for his Uncle Hosea's funeral services. When his mother died in 1987, her obituary had him listed as living in Haunville, LA. Searches of the Social Security Death Index do not reveal any record of him.

The following assumptions are made based on this author's research: He was born after the 1930 census and had at least one child as his mother is listed with seven grandchildren and only six are accounted for through his siblings' records.

II.1.D.A.5.C (4) (E) Irene Abernathy (30 September 1898 Calhoun County, AR- 13 June 1970 Butler County, MO)

Parents: Julian Rockett Abernathy and Lula Lenora Martin

She married Irvin Napoleon Williams (13 October 1892-June 1966 Dunklin County, MO) on 15 November 1914 in Harrell, AR. They were later divorced. They had five children: Herbert Everett, Virginia Elizabeth, Dorothy Marie, Irvin Lavern, and Imogene.

Her obituary appeared in the Malden (MO) Press-Merit, 18 June 1970. She is interred in Malden Memorial Cemetery in Dunklin County, MO.

II.1.D.A.5.C (4) (E) 1 Herbert Everett Williams (14 January 1917 Calhoun County, AR- 24 June 1918 Calhoun County, AR)

Parents: Irvin Napoleon Williams and Irene Abernathy

He is interred in Ricks Cemetery in Calhoun County.

II.1.D.A.5.C (4) (E) 2 Virginia Elizabeth Williams (b. 22 April 1919 Calhoun County, AR)

Parents: Irvin Napoleon Williams and Irene Abernathy

She married Nolan Travis Thomason (3 August 1917 Calhoun County, AR-13 February 1984 Cape Girardeau, MO) on 3 October 1936 in Calhoun County. Thomason has five children annotated for this couple. Nolan is interred in Malden Memorial Cemetery in Dunklin County, MO.

II.1.D.A.5.C (4) (E) 3 Dorothy Marie Williams (b. 17 October 1920 Calhoun County, AR)

Parents: Irvin Napoleon Williams and Irene Abernathy

She married Curtis Lee Thomason (3 October 1913 Calhoun County, AR-2 January 1995 Scott County, MO) on 26 December 1936 at Manila, MS. Thomason has one child annotated for this couple. Curtis is interred in Memorial Park Cemetery in Scott County, MO.

II.1.d.a.5.c (4) (E) 4 Irvin Lavern Williams (b. 5 November 1924 Calhoun County, AR)

Parents: Irvin Napoleon Williams and Irene Abernathy

He married Derosia Frances Parker (19 June 1923 Fulton County, KY-?) on 11 April 1942 in Dunklin County, MO. Thomason has two children annotated for this couple.

II.1.d.a.5.c (4) (E) 5 Imogene Williams (b. 8 September 1928 Calhoun County, AR)

Parents: Irvin Napoleon Williams and Irene Abernathy

She married Jack Russell (b. 17 December 1927 Shildler, OK) on 2 May 1945 in Paragould, AR. Thomason has two children annotated for this couple.

II.1.d.a.5.c (4) (F) Boyd Martin Abernathy (23 July 1901 Calhoun County, AR-12 September 1974 Malvern County, AR)

Parents: Julian Rockett Abernathy and Lula Lenora Martin

He is found in the 1930 census at Calhoun County, AR with a wife, four children and both in-laws. He married Bessie Adams (18 December 1902 Harrell, AR-May 1986 Malvern County, AR) on 25 July 1919. Their four children listed in the 1930 census are Robert, Martha, Bettie and Evelyn. Their first born child, Katherine A. (26 Apr 1921-7 August 1922), died as an infant and is interred in Ricks Cemetery in Calhoun County, AR. Additionally, Thomason has annotated six other children, born after the 1930 census.

Both Boyd and Bessie are interred in Ricks Cemetery.

II.1.d.a.5.c (4) (F) 1 Robert Byron Abernathy (b. 2 November 1922 AR)

Parents: Boyd Martin Abernathy and Bessie Adams

He married Helen Ashley (1 December 1928-March 1986) on 3 January 1948. They had five children per Thomason's documentation. Three survive and two are deceased: Patricia Ann (17 May 1949-29 April 1967) and Robert Byron, Jr. (7 May 1955-9 August 1955).

II.1.d.A.5.c (4) (F) 2 Martha Sue Abernathy (b. 4 January 1924 AR)

Parents: Boyd Martin Abernathy and Bessie Adams

She was married twice. Her first marriage was to Louis Henry Burgess (d. 10 May 1944 Lake Village, AR) on 13 November 1938. They had four children. Following Louis' death, she married his brother, Timothy John (b. 3 April 1924) on 1 March 1947. Martha and Timothy had one child. (Thomason)

II.1.d.A.5.c (4) (F) 3 Bettie Jo Abernathy (b. 18 May 1926 AR)

Parents: Boyd Martin Abernathy and Bessie Adams

She married Merrell H. Roberts (14 February 1921 AR-6 October 1993 Concordia, LA) on 8 May 1944. They had three children. (Thomason)

II.1.d.A.5.c (4) (F) 4 Evelyn Abernathy (b. 18 August 1927 Calhoun County, AR)

Parents: Boyd Martin Abernathy and Bessie Adams

She married Johnnie T. Wright (30 January 1919-25 May 2001) on 3 August 1944. They had two children. (Thomason)

II.1.d.A.5.c (4) (G) Gertrude Abernathy (2 December 1907 Calhoun County, AR-22 February 2003 Galveston County, TX)

Parents: Julian Rockett Abernathy and Lula Lenora Martin

She is located in the 1930 census at Calhoun County, AR with a spouse and three children. Gertrude married Thomas Daniel Ivy (15 January 1903 Calhoun County, AR-22 September 1972 LaMarque, TX) on 27 December 1924 in Calhoun County, AR. They had three children: James Rex, George Warren and Bobby D.

In the 1930 census, Thomas is annotated as "Dan" and the family rented a farm. Dan's brother, Larkin, also resided with the family in 1930. Thomas is interred in Campground Cemetery in Calhoun County.

Gertrude's obituary appeared in the *Galveston Daily News* on 24 February 2003.

Gertrude Abernathy Ivy, 95, of La Marque, passed away Saturday, February 22, 2003, at Mainland Medical Center in Texas City. Gertrude has been a resident of La Marque since 1948. She was born December 2, 1907, in Harrell, Arkansas, to Julian and Loula Abernathy. She was a member of the Highlands Baptist Church. Her parents, husband Dan T. Ivy, sons Bobby D. Ivy and James Rex Ivy all preceded her in death. Survivors include daughter-in-law Theresa Ivy of Texas City; son George Ivy and wife Billie, of Texas City; sisters Mamie Tims, of Smackover, Arkansas, and Mary Ruth Funk of Duncan, Michigan; sister-in-law Beatrice Ivy of Little Rock, Arkansas; brother-in-law Mack C. Ivy and wife Wanda of Santa Fe; six grandchildren and numerous nieces and nephews. Services will be held Tuesday February 25, 2003 from the James Crowder Funeral Home in La Marque with Brother Leo Smith officiating. Graveside service will be held Friday, February 28, 2003, at the Camp Ground Cemetery in Hampton, Arkansas.

II.1.d.a.5.c (4) (G) 1 James Rex Ivy (18 September 1925 Calhoun County, AR-13 July 1998 Galveston, TX)

Parents: Thomas Daniel Ivy and Gertrude Abernathy

August 1996: Texas City, Texas (per his brother, Bobby's obituary). His dates of birth and death were confirmed from Social Security Administration records.

II.1.d.a.5.c (4) (G) 2 George Warren Ivy (b. 1 March 1927 Calhoun County, AR)

Parents: Thomas Daniel Ivy and Gertrude Abernathy

August 1996: Texas City, Texas (per his brother, Bobby's obituary)

February 2003: Texas City, Texas (per his mother's obituary)

George Warren married Billie Reynolds and had three children: Douglas, Eva, and Gregory.

Douglas is married with a child named Julie.

Eva married Greg Gillespie. (Thomason)

II.1.d.A.5.c (4) (G) 3 Bobby D. Ivy (15 February 1930 Hampton, AR-23 August 1996 Galveston, TX)

Parents: Thomas Daniel Ivy and Gertrude Abernathy

Bobby's obituary appeared in the *Galveston Daily News* on 25 August 1996.

> *B.D. "Bob" Ivy, 66, of Texas City died Friday, August 23, 1996, in Texas City. Funeral services will be held Monday, August 26, 1996, at 10:00 a.m. in the Chapel of James Crowder Funeral Home in La Marque with Rev. Leo Smith officiating, burial to follow at the Forest Park East Cemetery in Webster. Mr. Ivy was born February 15, 1930, in Hampton, Arkansas. He was a retired production supervisor with Union Carbide, retiring after 37 years, a member of Highlands Baptist Church, veteran of the U.S. Air Force during the Korean War. Mr. Ivy is survived by his wife of 44 years, Theresa, of Texas City; mother, Gertrude Ivy of Texas City; one daughter, Susan LeBon of Highland Village, Texas; two sons Danny Ivy of Pasadena, Texas and Donald Ivy of Houston, Texas; three grandchildren, Adam Ivy, Erin Ivy, and Jared LeBon; two brothers Rex Ivy and George Ivy of Texas City.*

According to Gertrude's obituary, Theresa lived in Texas City, TX in February 2003.

Susan Ivy married Paul LeBon. They have one child named Jared. Danny Ivy's spouse is Carol. They have two children, Adam and Erin. Donald Ivy has no additional information to be shared. (Thomason)

II.1.d.A.5.c (4) (H) Edna Abernathy (13 September 1905 Calhoun County, AR-13 March 2001 Springhill, LA)

Parents: Julian Rockett Abernathy and Lula Lenora Martin

Edna seems to disappear after the 1920 census where she resided in her mother's residence. Thomason has her documented as married three times: Charles Shannon, Burr Evans, and Bill Bays. However, no 1930 census records turn up under her maiden name or any of those married names. She is mentioned in Hosea's 1983 obituary with the surname Evans and in Otis' 1987 obituary with the surname Bays. On both occasions, her residence is listed as Corpus Christi, TX.

II.1.D.A.5.C (4) (I) MARY RUTH ABERNATHY (B. 21 JULY 1910 CALHOUN COUNTY, AR)

Parents: Julian Rockett Abernathy and Lula Lenora Martin

She married O.B. Funk. Per her sister, Gertrude's, obituary in February 2003, she lived in Duncan, Michigan.

II.1.D.A.5.C (4) (J) MAMIE ABERNATHY (B. 1904 CALHOUN COUNTY, AR)

Parents: Julian Rockett Abernathy and Lula Lenora Martin

Mamie married a gentleman with the surname Timms. In the 1930 census, although listed in the residence of her mother, the last name is neither Abernathy nor Timms. The name appears to be Madison or Mullins. At the time of her sister, Gertrude's, death in February 2003 she resided in Smackover, AR.

II.1.D.A.5.C (4) (K) JACKSON DEAN ABERNATHY (28 JANUARY 1912-1 NOVEMBER 1935)

Parents: Julian Rockett Abernathy and Lula Lenora Martin

He died during military service.

II.1.D.A.5.C (5) ALLEN BURTON MARTIN, SR (8 JULY 1873-27 OCTOBER 1942 PINE BLUFF, AR)

Parents: Chesley Burton Martin and Martha Adeline Ware

He married Annie Watson (7 September 1881 Bradley County, AR-17 May 1923 Pine Bluff, AR) on 29 December 1901 in Bradley County, AR. According to the 1920 census, he, Annie and their seven children lived in Jefferson County, AR. They actually had eight children, but one died as an infant in 1907 and is interred in Graceland Cemetery in Pine Bluff, AR. Their other children were: Jeter Bell (November 1903 AR-July 1965 Houston, TX), Robert Ware (18 October 1904 AR-February 1969 Bradley County, AR), Ouida Helen (b. December 1905 AR), Allen Burton, Jr. (6 July 1909 AR-29 June 1953), James Chesley (11 March 1910-November 1931 Pine Bluff, AR), Glennie Elizabeth (8 June 1914 Pine Bluff, AR-18 December 1970 Los Angeles, CA), and Grace W (b. 1918 AR).

Following Annie's death, Allen remarried as he is annotated in the 1930 census at Jefferson County, AR with a wife named Bertha. From that census, Bertha's year of birth is estimated to be 1882 and she was born in Illinois. Bertha died in 1935.

Allen Burton Martin Sr.'s obituary from the *Pine Bluff Commercial* on Thursday 29 October 1942 follows. It was placed on file with the Arkansas History Commission in May 1991.

Funeral services for A.B. Martin, Sr., 69, resident of Pine Bluff since 1900 and operator of a dairy since 1917, who died Tuesday at his home on South Hazel will be held Friday morning at 10:30 o'clock from the Lakeside Methodist church, conducted by the Rev. R B Moore, pastor of the church, assisted by the Rev. E.C. Rule, pastor of First Methodist Church. Mr. Martin was born in Calhoun County, AR on July 8, 1873 son of the late Chesley and Adeline Ware Martin, pioneer residents of Arkansas. He came here in 1900 from Bradley County and was married in 1901 to the former Miss Annie Watson. She died in 1923. Mr. Martin was a member of the Lakeside Methodist Church.

He is survived by three sons, J. B. Martin of Houston, Tex., R. W. Martin of Pine Bluff, and A. B. Martin, Jr., stationed at Camp White, Ore., three daughters, Mrs. J. J. Rose of Pine Bluff, Mrs. B. P. Graves of Norfolk VA, and Mrs. C. E. Shell of Memphis; two brothers, R C. Martin of Pine Bluff and W. E. Martin of Warren; one sister, Mrs. Alice Marks of Houston, Tex.; five grandchildren and other relatives. Burial will be on the family lot in Bellwood cemetery in charge of Hoderness-South Mortuary. Active pallbearers: Troy Scallion, R B Cox; Bill Brewer, Charlie Whyte, Al Camp, Carl Johnson, C K Elliott, Walter Reed [husband of Dorothy Martin, niece of Allen Burton], and Louis Vick. Honorary pallbearers: A E Graves, A A. Province, M T Cutrell, J L Norton, R L Blankenship, Met Galligher, Garland Brewster, Will Simpson, RL McGhee, Ivy Scallion, W E Bobo, Bill Kennedy, Dr. O W Clark, and Stanley Dreyfus.

II.1.d.a.5.c (5) (A) Jeter Bell Martin (November 1903 AR-July 1965 Harris County, TX)

Parents: Allen Burton Martin, Sr and Annie Watson

Jeter was named for his father's boss. In the 1930 census, Jeter lived in Desha County, AR with a spouse and no children. He married Hester Davis and their year of marriage is estimated as 1927.

II.1.d.a.5.c (5) (B) Robert Ware Martin (18 October 1904 AR-8 February 1969 Bradley County, AR)

Parents: Allen Burton Martin, Sr and Annie Watson

He married Julia Milton Hoyle (9 December 1913 Bradley County, AR – 19 August 1987 Bradley County, AR). They had four children: Robert Ware II, Charles Allen, Helen Louise, and Elizabeth Anne.

The Warren Branch of the Southeast Arkansas Regional Library attempted to locate an obituary notice on Robert, Sr. but was unable to do so. The local funeral home, Frazer's Chapel of the Chimes, had no record on him either. However, he is interred in Oakland Cemetery in Warren, AR with his spouse Julia.

Julia's obituary appeared in *The Eagle Democrat* of Warren, AR on 26 August 1987.

Mrs. Julia Milton Hoyle Martin, age 73, of Warren, died Wednesday, August 19 at St. Vincent Infirmary in Little Rock. She was a daughter of the late Charlie T. and Etta Rowland Hoyle, and was born in Bradley County, December 9, 1913. Mrs. Martin was a retired nurse, a member of the First United Methodist Church, a member of the Red Bud Garden Club, and the widow of Robert Ware Martin. Survivors include two sons, Robert Ware Martin II of Solon, Ohio, Charles Allen Martin of Boise, Idaho; two daughters, Helen Louise "Judy" Austin of Nashville, Tennessee, Elizabeth Anne Martin Donaldson of Severna Park, Maryland; three sisters, Catherine Pirtle of Moro Bay, Mable Bethea of Hermitage, Anna Breeding of Little Rock, and seven grandchildren. The funeral service was held 10:30 a.m. Friday, August 21 at Frazer's Chapel of the Chimes with Rev. John Dill officiating. Organist was Janice Sullivan with Pam Reeves and Patsy Johnson providing special music. Burial was in Oakland Cemetery.

II.1.d.a.5.c (5) (C) Helen Ouida Martin (22 December 1905 Pine Bluff AR-9 August 1992 Pine Bluff AR)

Parents: Allen Burton Martin, Sr and Annie Watson

Helen was first married to Amon Fletcher in March 1924. He died 10 October 1927. In the 1930 census, she is annotated as widowed and listed under the Fletcher name. She and Amon had one daughter, Annie B, who is annotated in the 1930 census residing in the Allen Burton Martin, Sr household.

Her second spouse was John Joseph Rose (2 January 1901-August 1973 Pine Bluff, AR) whom she married in 1940. She is annotated as Mrs. J.J. Rose in her father's 1942 obituary and resided in Pine Bluff, AR.

Helen's obituary appeared in the *Pine Bluff Commercial* on 11 August 1992. At the time of her death, she was a resident of the Pine Bluff Nursing Home. She was educated at Pine Bluff and had lived there her entire life. She was a charter member of the Wesley United Methodist Church and served as church secretary for over 20 years. Graveside services were held at Graceland Cemetery on 12 August 1992 with Tom Hazelwood officiating.

Annie B. Fletcher (1926-1970), according to her mother's 1992 obituary, was married to a gentleman with the surname Jordan and that they had three children. One of her children was a male as Helen's obituary states she was preceded in death by a "grandson". Her other two children were listed in Helen's obituary as James Jordan of Pine Bluff and Sue Jordan Williams of Redfield, AR. Four great-grandchildren also survived.

II.1.D.A.5.C (5) (D) ALLEN BURTON MARTIN, JR (6 JULY 1909 AR-29 JUNE 1953 JEFFERSON COUNTY, AR)

Parents: Allen Burton Martin, Sr and Annie Watson

He served in the United States Army during World War II with the Tec 4, Ordinance Company. Thomason has documented that Allen, Jr. had a spouse by the first name of Polly. However, corroborating documentation has not been located.

According to an entry in the *Chesley Burton Martin Family Bible*, in the possession of Grace Martin Henshaw, Allen Jr. was murdered. His obituary appeared in the *Pine Bluff Commercial* on 30 June 1953. There were no survivors listed.

> *Funeral services for Allen Burton Martin, 43, of 5000 Hazel Street, a Jefferson county planter, who died Monday morning at the Davis hospital, will be held Wednesday afternoon at 4 o'clock in Robinson Chapel with Rev. John M. McCormack, pastor of Lakeside Methodist Church, officiating. Burial will be in Bellwood cemetery.*

II.1.D.A.5.C (5) (E) JAMES CHESLEY MARTIN (11 MARCH 1910 AR-NOVEMBER 1931 PINE BLUFF, AR)

Parents: Allen Burton Martin, Sr and Annie Watson

He died of pneumonia at the age of 21 and is buried in Graceland Cemetery in Jefferson County, AR.

II.1.d.a.5.c (5) (F) Elizabeth Glennie Martin (8 June 1914 Pine Bluff, AR-18 December 1970 Los Angeles, CA)

Parents: Allen Burton Martin, Sr and Annie Watson

Per her father's obituary in 1942, Elizabeth lived in Norfolk, VA. The obituary has her surname listed as Graves. She married Besley Pearson Graves. Her date of birth and death are confirmed through Social Security Administration records.

II.1.d.a.5.c (5) (G) Grace W. Martin (b. 1918 AR)

Parents: Allen Burton Martin, Sr and Annie Watson

Grace lived in Memphis, TN, per her father's 1942 obituary, with the surname of Shell. She resided in Garden Grove, CA in 1992, per her sister Helen's obituary, with the surname Henshaw.

II.1.d.a.5.c. (6) William Elbert Martin (14 July 1875-9 November 1943)

Parents: Chesley Burton Martin and Martha Adeline Ware
1900 census: Calhoun County, AR in the residence of his parents.
1920 census: Bradley County, AR with spouse. Occupation: farmer.
1942: Warren, AR (per his brother, Allen's obituary)
He married Labella Lee Hollingsworth (b. 1876 AR) and had one daughter, Elizabeth.

II.1.d.a.5.c. (7) Alice Ware Martin (28 April 1878-12 April 1962 Houston, TX)

Parents: Chesley Burton Martin and Martha Adeline Ware
1900 census: Calhoun County, AR in the residence of her parents.
She was apparently married twice. In her brother, Allen's, obituary from 1942 her surname was Marks. She was listed with the surname Bass in her brother, Robert's, obituary in 1961. The second spouse was Dr. Walter Bass.
From Walter Ware Bass (son of Alice Ware Martin Bass):

My mother spent two winters in Little Rock with her Uncle Tommy Ware while attending the local school. She also spent one or two winters in Fordyce with her sister, Ruth Wood, attending the Fordyce Training School where Sterling V. Wood taught. She also spent some time in Pine Bluff in the early days, doing some work and keeping house for her brothers, Allen Burton and Robert Chesley. Allen Burton worked for a man named Jeter in a wholesale merchandising store and later named his first son for him. Robert Chesley later moved to Watson Chapel and was employed by a cotton buyer.

II.1.D.A.5.C. (8) ROBERT CHESLEY MARTIN, SR (14 JULY 1882 CALHOUN COUNTY, AR-1961 PINE BLUFF, AR)

Parents: Chesley Burton Martin and Martha Adeline Ware

1900 census: Calhoun County, AR in the residence of his parents.

1930 census: Jefferson County, AR with wife, Bertie, and four children

He owned a residence valued at $4,000 and his listed occupation was a weigher for a cotton company. He was married twice as well. His first spouse was Eugenia Russell (b. 15 June 1886 Texarkana, TX) and they were wed in 1909 in Pine Bluff, AR. They had two children: Dorothy Delphne (b. 23 April 1911 Pine Bluff, AR) and George Chesley (1914 Pine Bluff, AR-1941 Cleveland, OH). His second spouse was Bertie Lee Owen (b. 6 April 1885 Lincoln County, AR) whom he married on 24 December 1919 in Pine Bluff, AR. Their children are obtained from his obituary in 1961.

Funeral services for Robert C. Martin, 79, who died Sunday at his home at Watson Chapel, were held today at Ralph Robinson and Son Mortuary by Rev Conrad N Glover of Sheridan and Rev G William Smith of Forest Park Baptist Church. Mr. Martin, for a number of years identified with the cotton business in Pine Bluff, was a native of Calhoun County. He was born July 14, 1882 son of the late Mr. and Mrs. Chesley Martin. He attended the schools in his native county and came to Pine Bluff in 1901. He was a cotton buyer and an employee of the Federal Compress Company prior to his retirement in 1948. He was a member of the Forrest Park Baptist Church.

Survivors include his wife, the former Bertie L Owen, one son, R C Martin Jr. of San Antonio TX, two daughters Mrs. Walter Reed of Pine Bluff and Mmrs. Clara Lee Becker of Chelmsford MA, one sister, Mrs. Alice Bass of Houston, TX; nine grandchildren and five great-grandchildren. Burial was in Bellwood Cemetery. Pallbearers were Claude Bobbitt, Chester Gordy, J D Covington, John Martin, Roy Jackson, Robert Rhodes and Harry Dean Rhodes. (Ralph Robinson and Son Mortuary)

II.1.d.A.5.c. (8) (A) Dorothy Delphne Martin
(b. 23 April 1912 Pine Bluff, AR)

Parents: Robert Chesley Martin, Sr and Eugenia Russell

1930 census: Jefferson County, AR in residence of father and stepmother

1961: Pine Bluff, AR (per father's obituary)

She married Walter Nixon Reed (30 May 1910 Rison, AR-24 March 1994 Jefferson County, AR). They met at Main Street Baptist Church in1929 and were married on 27 July 1930.

Grubaugh shares the following story:

> *Walter Nixon Reed was named Walter Vernon Reed but his middle name was changed to Nixon at age 1 1/2. The Reeds were farmers until 1920 when they moved to Pine Bluff. His mother's family had moved to Pine Bluff earlier. He attended school at Mead Schoolhouse and graduated from Pine Bluff High School in 1928. He drove a soda pop truck for Nehi Co. out of Little Rock and later for Cherry Cola Bottling Co.*
>
> *In 1943 he joined the Navy and went to boot camp in San Diego CA and then to Guam. He went to Guam on USS Crockett, a cruiser, and back on the USS Savo Island, a converted aircraft carrier. He was a dry land sailor working for the military postal service. In Nov 1944, he came home.*

From his 1994 obituary that appeared in the *Pine Bluff Commercial* on 26 March 1994, upon returning from the Navy, he was a salesman for Curtis Candy Company and was district supervisor for south Arkansas for many years. He then worked for Brown Packing Company, retiring in 1970.

Walter was a member of Olive Street Baptist Church where he served as deacon, Sunday School teacher and superintendent and sang in the choir. He is interred in Bellwood Annex Cemetery in Pine Bluff.

Children: Dale Nixon, Robert Russell, and Walter Neal

Dorothy was still living in April 2003, her 91st birthday, and contributed to this entry.

II.1.d.A.5.c. (8) (A) 1 Dale Nixon Reed
(b. 1931 Jefferson County, AR)

Parents: Walter Nixon Reed and Dorothy Delphne Martin

1994 residence: Houston, TX per father's obituary

II.1.D.A.5.C. (8) (A) 2 ROBERT RUSSELL REED (B. 1938 JEFFERSON COUNTY, AR)

Parents: Walter Nixon Reed and Dorothy Delphne Martin
1994 residence: Houston, TX per father's obituary

II.1.D.A.5.C. (8) (A) 3 WALTER NEAL REED (B. 1945 JEFFERSON COUNTY, AR)

Parents: Walter Nixon Reed and Dorothy Delphne Martin
1994 residence: Texarkana, TX per father's obituary

II.1.D.A.5.C. (8) (B) GEORGE CHESLEY MARTIN (1914 JEFFERSON COUNTY, AR-1941 CLEVELAND, OH)

Parents: Robert Chesley Martin, Sr and Eugenia Russell
1930 census: Jefferson County, AR in residence of father and stepmother.
He is interred in Riverside Cemetery in Cleveland.

II.1.D.A.5.C. (8) (C) ROBERT CHESLEY MARTIN JR (B. 21 FEBRUARY 1921 JEFFERSON COUNTY, AR)

Parents: Robert Chesley Martin, Sr and Bertie Lee Owen
1930 census: Jefferson County, AR in parents' residence
1961: San Antonio, TX per father's obituary
1992: Fayetteville, AR per wife, Enbe's, obituary
Robert Jr. was married twice: (1) Agnes Frances Rogers and (2) Enbe Woody (8 September 1925 Mitchell County, NC-24 August 1992 Washington County, AR).
Children of Robert and Agnes were Robert Chesley Martin III and a female child. Children of Robert and Enbe were George and Becky.
Enbe's obituary appeared in the *Northwest Arkansas Times* on 25 August 1992.

Enbe Martin, 66, of Fayetteville, died Monday, Aug. 24, 1992, at Washington Regional Medical Center. She was born September 8, 1925, at Bakersville, NC the daughter of N.B. and Maud Randolph Woody. She was a homemaker. A brother and three sisters preceded her in death. Survivors included: spouse, Robert C. Martin of the residence; a son, Dr. George C. Martin of McGehee; a daughter, Becky Sherwood of Fayetteville; three brothers, Otto Woody of Johnson City, TN; Byrk Woody of Limestone, TN and J.C. Woody of Brevard, NC; three sisters Nezzie Nesbitt of Van Wyck, SC; Esther Martin of Johnson City TN and Bassie Hood of Webster, FL; and six grandchildren. Funeral services were held at Moore's Chapel with the Rev. Gary C. Harrell officiating. Burial was at National Cemetery.

II.1.d.a.5.d. WILLIAM PHERIS MARTIN (1837 EDGEFIELD COUNTY, SC-27 MARCH 1872 CLAY COUNTY, AL)

Parents: James Franklin Martin and Margaret Walker
    1850 census: Edgefield County, SC in parents' residence
    1860 census: Talladega County, AL
    1870 census: Clay County, AL with a wife and three children (William, James and John).
    Spouse: Berthania E. Owens (1842 GA-1895 Clay County, AL).
    Military records on file:

> *Co I 30th AL Inf., CSA: Enlisted March 1, 1862 – Talladega, AL for 3 years. Was a POW captured at Champion Hill on May 16, 1863 by the Army of Tennessee and sent to Memphis, TN May 25, 1863. On June 29, 1863 was in a field near Vicksburg, MS. On June 30th he was at Camp Lee, VA and was exchanged July 4, 1863. He was evidently captured again because he appears on a Roll of Prisoners of War at Talladega AL May 22, 1865. He was paroled in Talladega AL.*

Marriage record on file: 17 January 1862, State of Alabama, Talladega County:

> *To any of the judges of said state any justice of the peace of this county or any other person legally authorized: These are to authorize you or either of you to solemnize the rites of matrimony between Wm. P Martin and Miss Berthania E. Owens of said county agreeably to the estate in such cares made and provided. Given at office of the Judge of Probate of said county this 27 January 1862, Wm. H. Thornton, Judge of Probate.*

> *In virtue of the above license, I have solemnized the rites of Matrimony between the above named persons, January 30, 1862. Wm. W. Watkins, JP*

There is some confusion as to what his spouse's given name was. In the 1870 census of Clay County, AL, taken on July 21, 1870, she is shown as being Burthinia. In her mother's probate in Union County, AR her name is listed as Bithania E. Martin. In her own probate records filed in Clay County, AL in 1895, she is shown as being Bethany E. Martin.

Children: William Samuel, James Wesley, John Thomas, Robert E. Lee, and Sanders Pheris. Upon William Pheris' death in 1872, his father was granted custodial rights to his minor children.

11 Sep 1882, per will of James Franklin Martin, William Pheris Martin's father; William Lackey named guardian of William Martin's minor children: James, John, William and Robert.

A newspaper citation indicates that he fell off a wagon and broke his neck. His probate records show he owned 400 acres of land just east of Ashland where the Google Earth map of today shows the "county country club" to be located. The land was valued at $2.50 to $3.33 per acre. Also, he owned two mules ($75 each), six cows ($190), 15 hogs and nine sheep. (Henshaw)

William Pheris Martin is interred in Olive Branch Cemetery in Clay County, AL.

II.1.D.A.5.D. (1) WILLIAM SAMUEL MARTIN
(B. 1864 CLAY COUNTY, AL)

Parents: William Pheris Martin and Berthania E. Owens
    1870 census: Clay County, AL in parents' residence
    1895: in his mother's probate shown as living in Camp County, TX
    1930 census: Wood County, TX with spouse, Martha, daughter, Lucius, and two grandchildren. They owned a farm.
    Two spouses: Mary E. Norton (b. November 1869 TX) and Martha _____ (b. 1876 MS). Martha's year of birth is estimated from the 1930 census.

II.1.D.A.5.D. (1) (A) LUCIUS A. MARTIN (B. 1905 MS)

Parents: William Samuel Martin and Martha _____
    1930 census: Wood County, TX residing with parents, children and annotated as widowed. Her last name was annotated as Munsey.
    Children: Elly G. Munsey (b. 1926 TX) and Eulide W. (b. 1927 TX)

II.1.D.A.5.D. (2) James Wesley Martin
(21 February 1866 Clay County, AL-16
September 1949 Clay County, AL)

Parents: William Pheris Martin and Berthania E. Owens

1870 census: Clay County, AL in parents' residence

1920 census: Clay County, AL with spouse, Aquilla (October 1867 AL-1926 Clay County AL), and children, Mary, Cora and James. They owned a farm

1930 census: Clay County, AL with children, William P., Katie M. (b. April 1891 Clay County, AL), Mary F. (b. November 1897 Clay County, AL), Era Mozelle (April 1901 Clay County, AL-07 September 1913 Clay County, AL), Cora L. (b. 1904 Clay County, AL) and James A.J. (b. 1907 Clay County, AL). James Wesley is listed as widowed.

Their only child for which substantial information has been located is William P.

II.1.D.A.5.D. (2) (A) William P. Martin (September 1889 Clay County, AL-01 November 1956 Clay County, AL)

Parents: James Wesley Martin and Aquilla A. Robertson

1930 census: Clay County, AL with spouse, Grace (29 October 1894 AL-January 1983 Clay County, AL), and three children: Mary (b. 1914 AL), Percy (18 September 1919 AL-12 February 1992 AL), and Opal E. (b. 1928 AL). The year of marriage for William and Grace is estimated to be 1910. His occupation is listed as a farmer.

No additional information has been found for Mary or Opal. Percy's year of birth and death were confirmed through Social Security Administration records.

II.1.D.A.5.D (3) John Thomas Martin (4 December 1867 Clay County, AL-20 January 1950 Bowie County, TX)

Parents: William Pheris Martin and Berthania E. Owens

1870 census: Clay County, AL – parents' residence

1930 census: Morris County, TX with spouse, Lydia Alice Gaither (6 January 1872 Clay County, AL-13 September 1950 Bowie County, TX). Owned residence valued at $600. No occupation was given for this individual. John and Lydia were married 13 December 1893 in Clay County, AL.

Children:

Prudie (December 1895 Clay County, AL-24 February 1984 Bowie County, TX)

Buren L. (May 1897 Clay County, AL-July 1967 Dallas County, TX)

Elizabeth aka Lizzie (February 1899 Clay County, AL-9 August 1983)

Blanca (30 April 1902 Bowie County, TX-25 February 1982 Taylor County, TX)

Flossie Mae (9 August 1904 Bowie County, TX-17 October 1905 Bowie County, TX)

John Pheris (5 June 1906 Upshur County, TX-March 1983 Bowie County, TX)

A.V. "Jack" (29 July 1907 Bowie County, TX-8 June 1920 Bowie County, TX)

This couple also had three infants who died the same day they were born.

II.1.D.A.5.D (4) ROBERT E. LEE MARTIN (1870 CLAY COUNTY, AL-BEFORE 1895)

Parents: William Pheris Martin and Berthania E. Owens

Robert is not mentioned as part of his mother's probate in 1895.

II.1.D.A.5.D (5) SANDERS PHERIS MARTIN (2 MARCH 1872 CLAY COUNTY, AL-31 AUGUST 1961 CLAY COUNTY, AL)

Parents: William Pheris Martin and Berthania E. Owens

Sanders was born three weeks prior to his father's accident and death.

He married Mary Fannie Phillips (21 February 1873 AL-16 September 1969 Clay County, AL) on 11 August 1895 in Clay County, AL.

1920 census: Clay County, AL with wife, Mary, and daughters, Grace, Lillian, Mary, and Sarah. They owned a farm.

1930 census: They remained in Clay County and had five children in the household: Eavy, Willie Grace, Lillian V., Mary W. and Sarah R.

Eavy (b. September 1896 Clay County, AL)

Willie Grace (b. February 1899 Clay County, AL) In the 1920 census, her occupation is listed as a public school teacher.

Lillian V. (b. 1902 Clay County, AL) In the 1920 census, her occupation is listed as a public school teacher.

Effie Lee (15 February 1905 Clay County, AL-22 October 1908 Clay County, AL)

Mary W. (b. 1901 Clay County, AL)

Sarah R. (b. 1913 Clay County, AL)

II.1.D.A.5.E. MARTHA MARTIN (1839 EDGEFIELD COUNTY, SC-1882 CLAY COUNTY, ALABAMA)

Parents: James Franklin Martin and Margaret Walker

There is a lone paragraph written about this individual in the book authored by L.L. Wood. The paragraph mentions that this couple had "no issue", meaning children, but extensive research of the census data from 1880 reveals that indeed they did have children - seven of them. The 1880 census finds Martha and husband, George, lived in Clay County, AL in the township of Ashland.

Martha was married to Dr. George N. Sims (1829 SC-30 January 1914 Jefferson County, AL).

In the 1880 census, George's occupation is listed as a physician and Martha's occupation is listed as keeping house. Children: Sylvester M., Martha J.C.A., George A., Mary F., John B., Emily J., and one other daughter whose name is not decipherable.

II.1.D.A.5.E. (1) SYLVESTER M. SIMS (1861 AL-26 MAY 1928 CLAY COUNTY, AL)

Parents: Dr. George N. Sims and Martha Martin

1880 census: Clay County, AL resided in parents' residence. Occupation: farmer.

1920 census: Coosa County, AL with spouse, Annie, and three children: George, Madelle and Peggie. Occupation: farmer

Sylvester married first Caroline Dunn (d. 31 December 1919 Etowah County, AL) on 15 November 1881 in Clay County, AL. Following Caroline's death, Sylvester married a second time to a woman, 21 years his junior, named Annie M. (25 July 1882 AL-15 May 1965 Jefferson County, AL).

II.1.D.A.5.E. (1) (A) GEORGE M. SIMS (B. 1904 AL)

Parents: Sylvester M. Sims and Caroline Dunn

1920 census: Coosa County, AL resided with his father and stepmother.

1930 census: Elmore County, AL – single/boarder

II.1.D.A.5.E. (1) (B) MADELLE SIMS (B. 1906 AL)

Parents: Sylvester M. Sims and Caroline Dunn

1920 census: Coosa County, AL resided with her father and stepmother.

II.1.D.A.5.E. (1) (C) Peggie Sims (b. 1908 AL)

Parents: Sylvester M. Sims and Caroline Dunn
    1920 census: Coosa County, AL resided with her father and stepmother.

II.1.D.A.5.E. (2) Martha J.C.A. Sims (1862 AL- 11 December 1950 Clay County, AL)

Parents: Dr. George N. Sims and Martha Martin
    1880 census: Clay County, AL – parents' residence
    1930 census: Clay County, AL with spouse, Charley, daughter, Kathryn N., and brother, John Benjamin. They owned a house valued at $2K. Kathryn's occupation is listed as a seamstress.
    Martha married Charley D. Harris (b. 1861 AL) on 11 January 1884 in Clay County, AL. Their marriage license has him listed as C.D. Harris.

II.1.D.A.5.E. (3) George A. Sims (1865 AL- 07 December 1953 Clay County, AL)

Parents: Dr. George N. Sims and Martha Martin
    1880 census: Clay County, AL resided with parents. Occupation: farm worker
    1930 census: Clay County, AL with spouse, Ida (24 June 1881 AL-15 November 1970 Talladega County, AL), and six children. Occupation: farmer.
    From the census, George and Ida's year of marriage is estimated as 1902.
    Children: Mozelle, George N., Annie P., Elsie M., Mildred, and Millard.
    Mildred and Millard were twins.
    Mozelle (1906 AL-11 February 1946 Calhoun County, AL) in the 1930 census, her occupation was listed as a saleswoman for a general store.
    George N. (b. 1908 AL) in the 1930 census, his occupation is listed as a salesman for a hardware store.
    Annie P. (b. 1912 AL)
    Elsie M. (b. 6 January 1915 AL)
    Mildred (b. 9 December 1920 AL)
    Millard (9 December 1920 AL-30 April 1995 Limestone County, AL)

I.1.D.A.5.E. (4) MARY F. SIMS (B. 1871 AL)

Parents: Dr. George N. Sims and Martha Martin
    1880 census: Clay County, AL resided with parents.

II.1.D.A.5.E. (5) JOHN BENJAMIN SIMS (B. 1873 AL)

Parents: Dr. George N. Sims and Martha Martin
    1880 census: Clay County, AL resided with parents.
    1930 census: Clay County, AL resided with his sister, Martha, and her spouse, Charley Harris.

II.1.D.A.5.E. (6) EMILY J. SIMS (B. 1876 AL)

Parents: Dr. George N. Sims and Martha Martin
    1880 census: Clay County, AL resided with parents.
    She married Fred Campbell on 22 March 1885 in Clay County, AL. He was 12 and she was nine.

II.1.D.A.5.F. HENRY HARRISON MARTIN (4 FEBRUARY 1841 EDGEFIELD COUNTY, SC-7 SEPTEMBER 1883 CLAY COUNTY, AL)

Parents: James Franklin Martin and Margaret Walker
    1880 census: Clay County, AL with wife, Sara Ann Bethany Bruce (b. 1847 Georgia). Occupation: farmer.
    Military Service: Company I, 14th Alabama Infantry, CSA. He was a member of the Masonic Order.
    Children: Eugenia, James Samuel, Mitchell Andrew, Dora, and Walter Alonza.
    Henry is interred in Olive Branch Church Cemetery near Ashland, AL

II.1.d.a.5.f. (1) Eugenia L. Martin (1867 AL-07 January 1946 Clay County, AL)

Parents: Henry Harrison Martin and Sara Ann Bethany Bruce

She married William M. Riley (1866 AL-14 July 1945 Clay County, AL) on 18 January 1888 in Clay County, AL.

1880 census: Clay County, AL resided with parents.

1930 census: Clay County, AL with spouse, William, and three children. Occupation: proprietor of a café.

Children: John T. (b. 1906 AL), Ethel B. (b. 1908 AL), and Dora (b. 1910 AL). The children's years of birth are estimated from the 1930 census. John's occupation in 1930 is listed as a farmer.

II.1.d.a.5.f. (2) James Samuel Martin (27 February 1869 AL-21 June 1951 Chambers County, AL)

Parents: Henry Harrison Martin and Sara Ann Bethany Bruce

James married Vandora Fetner (1870 AL-before 1951) in 1886.

1930 census: Chambers County, AL with spouse, Vandora, and two children. Occupation: cotton mill carpenter. They rented their residence for $3 per month.

Children: Bertha, Myrtle T., Estelle, Ruby, W.H., Manning, Omar, and Hurley.

James Samuel's obituary appeared in the LaGrange, Georgia *Daily News* on 23 June 1951.

> *James Samuel Martin died in Fairfax on Thursday, June 21. Funeral services will be held Saturday afternoon at the New Harmony Christian Church in Clay County, Alabama. The Rev. J.W. Chambers, assisted by the Rev. N.A. Long, will conduct the services. Surviving are Mr. Martin's four daughters: Mrs. Bertha Wills of LaGrange, GA; Mrs. Myrt King of Atlanta, GA; Miss Estelle Martin of LaGrange; Mrs. Ruby Lindsey of Atlanta; four sons: W.H. Martin of Fairfax, Ala.; Manning Martin of Lineville, Ala.; Omar Martin of Oxford, Ala.; Hurley Martin of Fairfax.*

II.1.d.a.5.f. (2) (A) Bertha Martin

Parents: James Samuel Martin and Vandora Fetner

1951: LaGrange, GA per father's obituary

II.1.D.A.5.F. (2) (B) Myrtle T. Martin (2 January 1895 AL-9 March 1988 Stephens County, GA)

Parents: James Samuel Martin and Vandora Fetner

1930 census: Chambers County, AL resided in her parents' residence with sons, Charles (b. 1924 AL) and James (b. 1926 AL), annotated as widowed and employed in a cotton textile mill.

1951 Atlanta, GA per her father's obituary.

From the 1930 census, her father's obituary and her death certificate Myrtle's married name was King. In the 1930 census it appears that her first son, Charles, has "Jr." behind his name. But, the writing is too difficult to read in order to make that determination confidently.

II.1.D.A.5.F. (2) (C) Estelle Martin (30 May 1908 AL-21 February 1993 Jefferson County, AL)

Parents: James Samuel Martin and Vandora Fetner

1930 census: Chambers County, AL resided with parents. Occupation: cotton textile mill.

1951: LaGrange, GA per father's obituary

Estelle never married.

II.1.D.A.5.F. (2) (D) Ruby Martin

Parents: James Samuel Martin and Vandora Fetner

1951: Atlanta, GA per father's obituary and annotated as "Lindsey"

II.1.D.A.5.F. (2) (E) W.H. Martin (B. 1887 AL)

Parents: James Samuel Martin and Vandora Fetner

1930 census: Chambers County, AL with spouse, Mary, and two daughters. The family was living next door to his parents. Occupation: cotton textile mill. They rented a home for $4 per month.

1951: Fairfax, AL per father's obituary

Children: Agnes and Lillian. Their ages are too difficult to decipher in the 1930 census to estimate a year of birth.

Not knowing what the initials "W.H." stands for has made locating additional data hard.

II.1.D.A.5.F. (2) (F) MANNING MARTIN (1890 AL-1973 AL)

Parents: James Samuel Martin and Vandora Fetner
    1930 census: Clay County, AL with spouse, Edna (28 March 1892 AL-October 1977 Jefferson County, AL), and three children. Occupation: farmer. Their estimated year of marriage is 1918.
    1951: Lineville, AL per father's obituary
    Children: Zula (b. 1920 AL), Howell (b. 1922 AL) and Hazell (b. 1925 AL).

II.1.D.A.5.F. (2) (G) OMAR MARTIN (1897 AL-AUGUST 1957 AL)

Parents: James Samuel Martin and Vandora Fetner
    1930 census: Lawrence County, AL with spouse, Pearl, and two daughters. Occupation: farmer. Their estimated year of marriage is 1921.
    1951: Oxford, AL per father's obituary
    Children: Annie P. (b. 1924 AL) and Margarette (b. 1925 AL).

II.1.D.A.5.F. (2) (H) HURLEY MARTIN (26 JULY 1895 AL-JUNE 1976 CHAMBERS COUNTY, AL)

Parents: James Samuel Martin and Vandora Fetner
    1951: Fairfax, AL per father's obituary
    No census listing or spouse/children have been located for this individual. His dates of birth and death were confirmed from Social Security Administration records.

II.1.D.A.5.F. (3) MITCHELL ANDREW MARTIN (26 FEBRUARY 1872 CLAY COUNTY, AL-30 MAY 1937 CLAY COUNTY, AL)

Parents: Henry Harrison Martin and Sara Ann Bethany Bruce
    1930 census: Clay County, AL with a spouse and no children. Occupation: farmer.
    Woodson has annotated two spouses for Mitchell: Ann McCormick and a Mrs. Bailey (believed to be Henrietta). However, the name of his spouse appearing in the 1930 census is poorly written and does not appear to be either of those names.
    Mitchell is interred in Olive Branch Church Cemetery in Ashland, AL.

II.1.D.A.5.F. (4) DORA MARTIN (MARCH 1873 AL-1948 AL)

Parents: Henry Harrison Martin and Sara Ann Bethany Bruce

1930 census: Clay County, AL with spouse, Garrison, and seven children. Their occupation was listed as farmers and they owned a farm.

She married Garrison Fetner (1869 AL-1934 AL), brother of James Samuel's spouse, on 22 July 1888.

Children:

Francis (b. 1901 AL)

Mary E. (b. 1904 AL)

Deone (b. 1908 AL) occupation in 1930: farmer

Thelma (b. 1910 AL)

Theola (b. 1913 AL)

Woodroe (b. 1914 AL)

Chipley (b. 1918 AL)

II.1.D.A.5.F. (5) WALTER ALONZA MARTIN (13 DECEMBER 1877 AL-1915 CLAY COUNTY, AL)

Parents: Henry Harrison Martin and Sara Ann Bethany Bruce

Walter married Lula R. Owen (February 1875 AL-1952 Clay County, AL) on 28 November 1895 in Clay County, AL.

In the 1920 census of Clay County, AL are his spouse, Lula, and three daughters. Lula is annotated as widowed. The family rented a farm and Lula's annotated occupation is farmer.

Children: Louzelle (b. 1907 AL), Etta Maud (b. 1910 AL) and Cordia Cila (b. 1913 AL).

II.1.D.A.5.G. SAMUEL BUD MARTIN (1843 EDGEFIELD COUNTY, SC-1880 CLAY COUNTY, AL)

Parents: James Franklin Martin and Margaret Walker

He had no spouse or children. Samuel died at Selma, AL of complications from injuries sustained during the Civil War.

II.1.D.A.5.H. SANDERS M. MARTIN (10 MARCH 1846 EDGEFIELD COUNTY, SC –26 JANUARY 1916 CLAY COUNTY, AL)

Parents: James Franklin Martin and Margaret Walker

    1880 census: Clay County, AL

    1900 census: Clay County, AL

    1910 census: Clay County, AL

Sanders married first, Lydia V. Bruce (11 August 1845 GA- 5 January 1879 Clay County, AL) about 1868. She is interred in New Harmony Christian Church Cemetery in Cragford, AL. He married secondly, Tiny Clementine McCormick (1846-April 1916 Clay County, AL).

Tiny's obituary quoted from *Lineville Headlight* of April 28, 1916:

> *Mrs. Sanders [Dink] Martin an excellent woman of the New Harmony community died at her home last week and her remains were laid to rest beside those of her husband, who died two or three months ago. The deceased was a woman of many admirable traits, character and will be greatly missed in the community where she lived so long.*

Sanders enlisted in the CSA army at Selma, Talladega County, Alabama on 28 Jan 1864 at age 16 as a private. As the story goes, his mother insisted he come home and he was furloughed until 1 Feb 1864. He was assigned to Holtsclaw Brigade upon his return from furlough.

Later that year, he was assigned to "Lockhart's Battalion", organized in Selma, which was later renamed the 62nd Alabama Infantry Regiment, Mobile Company G. This regiment was more commonly known as Sam Morgan Cadets. Wounded in the arm, Sanders was admitted to Ross Hospital at Mobile, Alabama on Nov. 18, 1864, suffering intermittent fever. He was transferred to General Hospital at Mobile, November 30, 1864 when he was determined not to be making progress in the healing process. He was discharged from medical care in February 1865 and returned to battle.

Captured at Fort Blakely, Alabama on April 9, 1865, he was imprisoned at Ship Island, Mississippi. Transferred at Vicksburg, Mississippi for exchange, he was received at Camp Townsend on May 6, 1865 by a Confederate agent. When he was finally discharged at Mobile, Alabama, it is said that he threw his musket and ammunition into Mobile Bay and stated he did not want them in his way on his trip back home. (Woodson)

Obituary quoted from *Lineville Headlight* of Feb 4, 1916:

> *Mr. Sanders Martin, familiarly known as "Dink" died at his home, six miles east of Lineville, Wednesday morning, Jan. 26 after an illness of a week. Pneumonia was the malady from which he died. A widow and nine children survive him. The deceased was 69 years of age and was a member of the New Harmony Christian Church. His remains were laid to rest at New Harmony Thursday January 27.*

II.1.D.A.5.H. (1) CHESLEY BURTON MARTIN (29 JULY 1869 CLAY COUNTY, AL-16 NOVEMBER 1949 CLAY COUNTY, AL)

Parents: Sanders M. Martin and Lydia V. Bruce

   1880 census: Clay County, AL resided with parents.

   1920 census: Chambers County, AL. Occupation: minister and farmer.

   1930 census: Bibb County, AL. He rented the family residence for $12 a month. Occupation: Baptist minister.

   From *Martins of Martin's Mill of South Carolina* p. 58:

Chesley B. Martin . . . trusted the Lord for salvation in March 1878, while his mother, with her children gathered close about her, was praying to our Heavenly Father to protect her and her little ones from disaster. During his early life he spent much of his time studying the New Testament. Although his parents were members of a Methodist Church, his understanding of the teachings of God's Word lead him to become a Baptist. At the age of 17 he put on Christ in open confession and baptism, uniting with Mt. Gilead Baptist Church and was baptized by Rev. Jesse Robinson. This church was located in Randolph Co [AL] two miles west of Blake's Ferry on what was then known as the Wedowee and Lineville Road.

He was married to Martha E. Knight in November 1890. He wanted to do something to help suffering humanity, so he studied medicine. He and his wife moved from Clay County to Marian County and in 1895 moved to Lee County, MS. In November 1898 they came back to Clay County.

In September 1899 he received consciously and very definitely a call from the Lord to become His Gospel Messenger here on earth. On Saturday before the third Sunday in August 1900 Salem Baptist Church, located at Wasabulga in Clay County near Cragford, declared him a licensed Minister.

After one or two months he attended a worship service at New Harmony Christian Church where his father and father-in-law and other members of their families were present. Whereupon C B Martin's father and father-in-law said to him that it was a good time for him to make a start. It seemed very fitting for him to preach his first sermon to his own kin. Through the counsel and advice of Rev. C L Harris and Rev. J R Stosdghill he went to school again for a few months. Taking correspondence courses, attending Bible conferences and private, prayerful study of the Bible he obtained his theological training.

Chesley Burton was married twice. His first spouse was Martha E. Knight (10 February 1872 Clay County, AL-21 March 1934 Randolph County, AL). Chesley and Martha were married on 1 November 1890 in Clay County, AL. She is interred in Lincoln, AL.

Following Martha's death, Chesley remarried in 1936 to Cora Barfield (22 February 1880 Randolph County, AL-3 October 1967 Clay County, AL). Cora is interred in the Old City Cemetery in Lineville, AL.

Martha and Chesley had 11 children: Hattie Viola, Edna Iola, Lydia Charlotte, David Sanders, Lillie Eliza Clementine, Ethel, William Ethridge, Charles Barnett, John Lysle, Nonnie, and Clarence Chesley. He and Cora had no children.

He is interred in the First Baptist Church Cemetery in Roanoke, AL where his daughter Nonnie is also buried.

II.1.d.A.5.H. (1) (A) Hattie Viola Martin (13 October 1891 Clay County, AL-13 December 1891 Randolph County, AL)

Parents: Chesley Burton Martin and Martha E. Knight

II.1.d.A.5.H. (1) (B) Edna Iola Martin (13 September 1893 Marion County, AL-)

Parents: Chesley Burton Martin and Martha E. Knight

Edna was wed to Emmett M. Neely (1868 AL-03 July 1957 Coosa County, AL) in August 1913 in Troup County, GA.

1930 census: Randolph County, AL with spouse and six children. Spouse's occupation: cotton mill worker. They rented their home for $180 a month.

Children: Bobby, Lee, Betty, Charley, Austin, and Burton

Edna was not listed as a survivor in her brother, David's, 1987 obituary.

II.1.d.A.5.H. (1) (B) 1 Bobby Neely (b. 1913 GA)

Parents: Emmett M. Neely and Edna Iola Martin

1930 census: Randolph County, AL resided with parents. Occupation: cotton mill worker.

He was not mentioned as a survivor in brother, Austin's, 1986 obituary.

II.1.D.A.5.H. (1) (B) 2 Lee Neely (b. 1917 GA)

Parents: Emmett M. Neely and Edna Iola Martin
  1930 census: Randolph County, AL resided with parents.
  1986: Lincoln, Nebraska per Austin's obituary

II.1.D.A.5.H. (1) (B) 3 Betty Neely (b. 1918 GA)

Parents: Emmett M. Neely and Edna Iola Martin
  1930 census: Randolph County, AL resided with parents.
  1986: Alex City, AL per Austin's obituary with surname as Brown.

II.1.D.A.5.H. (1) (B) 4 Charley Neely (b. 1922 GA)

Parents: Emmett M. Neely and Edna Iola Martin
  1930 census: Randolph County, AL resided with parents.
  1986: Roswell, NM per Austin's obituary. In the obituary, her first name was spelled Charlie.

II.1.D.A.5.H. (1) (B) 5 Austin Neely (25 April 1924 GA-25 February 1986 Meriwether County, GA)

Parents: Emmett M. Neely and Edna Iola Martin
  1930 census: Randolph County, AL resided with parents.
  Children: none although a foster child is listed in his obituary.
  Austin's obituary was published in the *Manchester Star-Mercury* on 5 March 1986. His funeral service was held from St. James United Methodist Church with Rev. J.R. McAiley officiating. Burial was in Cedarwood Cemetery in Roanoke, AL. He worked as a parts manager, was a war veteran and a member of the St. James United Methodist Church. His wife Lillian survived him.

II.1.D.A.5.H. (1) (B) 6 BURTON NEELY (B. 1927 GA)

Parents: Emmett M. Neely and Edna Iola Martin
    1930 census: Randolph County, AL resided with parents.
    1986: Alex City, AL per Austin's obituary (annotated as Bert)

II.1.D.A.5.H. (1) (C) LYDIA CHARLOTTE MARTIN (B. 3 MARCH 1895 MARION COUNTY, AL)

Parents: Chesley Burton Martin and Martha E. Knight
    She married William T. Cate on 25 December 1913 in Troup County, GA.
    Lydia was not listed as a survivor in her brother, David's, 1987 obituary.

II.1.D.A.5.H. (1) (D) DAVID SANDERS MARTIN (8 MAY 1897 LEE COUNTY, MS-17 OCTOBER 1987 ALACHUA COUNTY, FL)

Parents: Chesley Burton Martin and Martha E. Knight
    1920 census: Troup County, GA - Boarder/single/shipping clerk.
    1930 census: Troup County, GA with spouse, Lena, and son. They owned a house valued at $5000. Occupation: assistant manager automobile company. Residence: 106 Hill Street.
    David served in the U.S. Navy in the hospital corps during WWI.
    He married, first, Lena Walker (26 September 1901 GA-January 1985 Broward County, FL) on 8 August 1926 in LaGrange, GA. They had one son, William C. His second wife was Erma C. Fowler. Erma survived David, and at the time of his death, was residing in Hawthorne, FL.
    David's obituary appeared in the *Gainesville Sun* on 19 October 1987:

> *David Sanders Martin died at the age of 90 at the Veterans Administration Medical Center in Gainesville, FL on October 17, 1987. He moved from LaGrange, GA to Hawthorne, FL in 1979 following retirement. Mr. Martin was a retired real estate broker who had served as a member of both the LaGrange and Georgia tax boards. Having served in the U.S. Navy in World War I, he was chosen as a member of the Selective Service Board of Defense during World War II. David was a member of the American Legion, Shrine Club, Elks Club, F&AM Union Lodge No. 28 and the First Baptist Church of LaGrange. Nationally, he had been a member of the United Nations Association of the United States, National Voter Advisory Board and the*

American Security Council. He was listed in, among other publications, "Who's Who in the South and Southwest" and "Who's Who in Commerce and Industry."

According to the obituary, his wife, Erma, five daughters, one son, sister, Ethyl Breed, and three grandchildren survived him. A letter from June Underwood, dated 12 September 2003, explains the connection of the five daughters, which were undocumented until his obituary. Mrs. Underwood writes,

> *My stepmother, Erma, married David Martin. Lelia and Pearl were my full sisters. Edna is my stepsister; she was Erma's daughter by her first marriage to my father. Lorraine is my half-sister; we have the same Daddy. Not one of us is blood kin to this Martin family.*

So per Mrs. Underwood's letter, David Sanders Martin only had the one son as is consistent with history up until his death.

II.1.D.A.5.H. (1) (D) 1 WILLIAM CLAYTON MARTIN (4 FEBRUARY 1927 GA-13 SEPTEMBER 2001 LEVY, FL)

Parents: David Sanders Martin and Lena Walker

1930 census: Troup County, GA resided with parents.

1987: Atlanta, GA (per father's obituary)

William's obituary appeared in the *Levy County Journal* on 20 September 2001. He was the owner of Martin's Country Store in Otter Creek. He was a Mason, a medic in the U.S. Army in World War II and a member of the First Baptist Church in Inglis, FL. His obituary stated, "he was a good family man and a hard worker." Interment was in Dunnellon Memorial Gardens.

From his obituary, he had a spouse, Betty, and two sons, William Clayton, Jr. and James Harold.

II.1.D.A.5.H. (1) (E) LILLIE ELIZA CLEMENTINE MARTIN (B. 17 MARCH 1899 CLAY COUNTY, AL)

Parents: Chesley Burton Martin and Martha E. Knight

She married James Bruce Breed (29 May 1896 AL-February 1967 AL) in Troup County, GA 12 February 1916.

1930 census: Chambers County, AL Occupation: cotton mill worker. Rented house for $3 a month.

Children: Lewis C. (13 May 1917 AL-31 July 1989 Carteret County, NC), James P. (9 October 1919 AL-12 February 1995 Chambers County, AL), Sybil (b. 1923 AL), Hilton H. (b. 1926 AL) and Nonnie (b. January 1930 AL).

Lillie was not listed as a survivor in her brother, David's, 1987 obituary.

II.1.D.A.5.H. (1) (F) ETHEL MARTIN (23 JANUARY 1902 RANDOLPH COUNTY, AL-31 MARCH 1988 TALLADEGA COUNTY, AL)

Parents: Chesley Burton Martin and Martha E. Knight

She married Johnny Breed (b. 1885 AL) in Chambers County, AL on 8 April 1917.

In 1930, the couple and six daughters lived in Randolph County, AL where Johnny was a cotton mill worker and they rented their home for $240 a month. Their children were: Mary Beth (b. 1921 AL), Mildred (b. 1923 AL), Sara P. (b. 1924 AL), Lois V. (b. May 1927 AL), Martha (b. October 1929 AL) and Tabitha (b. October 1929 AL). Other than being able to estimate each daughter's date of birth from the 1930 census, no other data has been found for this family.

According to her brother, David's, obituary, Ethel lived in Childersburg, AL.

II.1.D.A.5.H. (1) (G) WILLIAM ETHRIDGE MARTIN (16 JULY 1904 RANDOLPH COUNTY, AL-23 AUGUST 1907 RANDOLPH COUNTY, AL)

Parents: Chesley Burton Martin and Martha E. Knight

His cause of death was entered as spinal meningitis on the death certificate and he is interred in Mount Prospect Baptist Church cemetery in Ophelia, AL.

II.1.D.A.5.H. (1) (H) CHARLES BARNETT MARTIN (B. 25 DECEMBER 1906 RANDOLPH COUNTY, AL)

Parents: Chesley Burton Martin and Martha E. Knight

1920 census: Chambers County, AL in parents' residence.

Military service: U.S. Merchant Marine. Rank: captain.

Charles was not listed as a survivor in his brother, David's, 1987 obituary.

II.1.D.A.5.H. (1) (I) JOHN LYSLE MARTIN (B. 10 JULY 1909 RANDOLPH COUNTY, AL)

Parents: Chesley Burton Martin and Martha E. Knight
    1920 census: Chambers County, AL in parents' residence
    John is the twin of Nonnie.
    John was not listed as a survivor in his brother, David's, 1987 obituary.

II.1.D.A.5.H. (1) (J) NONNIE MARTIN (10 JULY 1909 RANDOLPH COUNTY, AL-24 JULY 1909 ROANOKE, AL)

Parents: Chesley Burton Martin and Martha E. Knight
    She is the twin of John Lysle and is interred in the First Baptist Church cemetery of Roanoke, AL.

II.1.D.A.5.H. (1) (K) CLARENCE CHESLEY MARTIN (7 JULY 1912 FRANKLIN, GA-AUGUST 1982 SHELBY COUNTY, AL)

Parents: Chesley Burton Martin and Martha E. Knight
    Clarence married Helen Roland (29 June 1912 West Blocton, AL-30 December 1993 Shelby County, AL) on 25 March 1934.
    1920 census: Chambers County, AL in parents' residence
    1930 census: Bibb County, AL in parents' residence
    Military service: WWII
    Children: none known
    From *Martins of Martin's Mill of South Carolina* p. 62:

> *...made his home there [West Blocton, AL]. Engaged with his father-in-law in distribution of pure oil, gasoline and oil products; also in the retail gas and oil business. They also operate an undertaking business, together with a burial life insurance agency. He entered the armed services of his country in November 1942.*

II.1.d.a.5.h (2) Henry Lucious Waits Martin (b. 24 April 1871 Clay County, AL)

Parents: Sanders M. Martin and Lydia V. Bruce
    1880 census: Clay County, AL – parents' residence
    No other census listings were located.
    Spouse unknown.
    Researchers Boswell and Woodson have annotated three children for this gentleman: Wesley Sanders, Gertrude Lynch and Mae Brock. Extensive searches did not corroborate that information.

II.1.d.a.5.h (3) Nancy Idella Martin (b. 19 July 1873 Clay County, AL)

Parents: Sanders M. Martin and Lydia V. Bruce
    1880 census: Clay County, AL in parents' residence
    She married William W. Nolen on 27 December 1896 in Clay County, AL.
    In the 1910 census, Nancy resided with her parents in Clay County. The census listing had her widowed with three children: Limon Beecher (b. 1898 AL), Stella (b. 1903 AL) and Willie (b. 1906 AL). After 1910, no subsequent census listings were located for Nancy or the children. Other genealogists have recorded a fourth child as Bela, but no evidence has been found to support the existence of such a child.
    Woodson (1980), reported Nancy as living as late as 1971.

II.1.d.a.5.h (4) Eliza Cornelia Martin (22 September 1875 Clay County, AL-22 July 1946)

Parents: Sanders M. Martin and Lydia V. Bruce
    In both the 1880 and 1900 censuses, Eliza is living with her parents in Clay County, AL.
    She married John H. Farrell (b. 1863 AL) in 1902.
    1930 census: Meriwether County, GA with spouse, John, and three children. Occupation: farmer. Their children listed were: Glen Webster (b. 1914 AL), Weebe (b. 1919 AL) and Wayne (b. 1913 AL). Other researchers have listed a child named Wayne Weebe, but the 1930 census clearly lists both males separately.

II.1.d.a.5.h (5) James Ransom Martin (1 November 1877 Clay County, AL-25 December 1901 Clay County, AL)

Parents: Sanders M. Martin and Lydia V. Bruce
    1880 and 1900 censuses: Clay County, AL in parents' residence

II.1.d.a.5.h (6) Robert Allen Martin (b. May 1884 Clay County, AL)

Parents: Sanders M. Martin and Clementine McCormick
    1900 census: Clay County, AL in parents' residence
    Woodson reports two spouses for this gentleman: Jessie Bowman and Ida Cooper. A search of records does not reveal any additional information other than that reported previously by Woodson in 1980. She wrote that Robert had no children.

II.1.d.a.5.h (7) Laura Jane Martin (10 March 1885 Clay County, AL-12 March 1928 Clay County, AL)

Parents: Sanders M. Martin and Clementine McCormick
    1900 and 1910 censuses: Clay County, AL in parents' residence
    1920 census: Clay County, AL with spouse, Ernest C. DeVaughn (1886 AL-09 August 1958 Clay County, AL), and daughter, Juanita. Occupation: farmer.
    1930 census: no listing found
    Children: Bobby and Juanita (b. 1917 AL). Grubaugh has documented that Bobby married Irma Adamson. Juanita has been married twice: Harvey Moore and James Crews.

II.1.d.a.5.h (8) Martha Luellen Martin (22 September 1887 Clay County, AL-December 1975 Talladega County, AL)

Parents: Sanders M. Martin and Clementine McCormick
    1900 census: Clay County, AL in parents' residence
    1920 census: Clay County, AL with spouse, Northern, and two daughters. Occupation: farmer.

1930 census: Clay County, AL with spouse, Northern, and two daughters. Occupation: blacksmith. They owned their house and an iron works shop. From the census, their year of marriage is estimated to be 1910.

Children: Vinnie and Vergie.

II.1.D.A.5.H (8) (A) VINNIE ORR (14 NOVEMBER 1909 AL-27 FEBRUARY 2002 JEFFERSON COUNTY, AL)

Parents: Northern Orr and Martha Luellen Martin

In both the 1920 and 1930 censuses, Vinnie is listed in her parents' Clay County, AL household. In 1930, her occupation is listed as a telephone operator.

Spouse: Alton Campbell (Grubaugh)

II.1.D.A.5.H (8) (B) VERGIE ORR (B. 1915 AL)

Parents: Northern Orr and Martha Luellen Martin

1920 and 1930 censuses: Clay County, AL in parents' residence.

Spouse: T. Jeff Clark (Grubaugh)

II.1.D.A.5.H (9) LULA BESS MARTIN (16 FEBRUARY 1892 CLAY COUNTY, AL-JULY 1973 MONTGOMERY, AL)

Parents: Sanders M. Martin and Clementine McCormick

1900 and 1910 censuses: Clay County, AL in parents' residence

Lula married Frank Barlow (7 December 1886 AL-February 1969 Montgomery, AL) in 1921.

In 1930, she and Frank lived in Montgomery where he worked as a loan company manager. In that year's census, she is annotated as Bessie.

Their one child died as an infant. (Grubaugh)

II.1.D.A.5.H (10) WYATT SANDERS MARTIN (B. SEPTEMBER 1889 CLAY COUNTY, AL)

Parents: Sanders M. Martin and Clementine McCormick

1900 and 1910 census: Clay County, AL in parents' residence.

Spouse: Marion Peters (Grubaugh)

II.1.d.a.5.h (11) John Tyler Martin (22 March 1893 Clay County, AL-15 July 1967 Etowah County, AL)

Parents: Sanders M. Martin and Clementine McCormick

1900 and 1910 census: Clay County, AL in parents' residence.

1920 census: Clay County, AL with spouse, Lexie (31 August 1897 AL-14 September 1994 Comanche County, OK). Occupation: farmer.

II.1.d.a.5.i. James Allen Martin (9 March 1848 Edgefield County, SC-2 July 1895 Calhoun County, AR)

Parents: James Franklin Martin and Margaret Walker

1880 census: Calhoun County, AR

A bizarre circumstance surrounding this gentleman is the similarity in dates relating to his two spouses. Both wives shared the same birthday and died one year to the day of each other. Both are buried alongside him, although he and his first spouse had been divorced for over 40 years at the time of her death. This created a need for this author to visit the cemetery to see how accurate these dates were and found them to be true as far as the inscription on the actual tombstones.

He married first, Loula West (10 October 1846 Alabama-28 October 1921 Calhoun County, AR). He married second, Lucinda Hanna (10 October 1846 AR-28 October 1922 Calhoun County, AR) on 13 January 1876. Both Loula and Lucinda are buried at Ricks Cemetery in Calhoun County, AR.

He and Loula had one child named Mink, and he and Lucinda had two children named Dora and Jimmy.

The second story related to this relative is the circumstances surrounding his death, which is relayed by the following letter from Alice Martin [Ware] to her uncle Sanders Martin.

Transcript of a letter from Alice Martin, daughter of Chesley Burton Martin, she wrote at the age of 17:

Summerville, Ark

My Dear Uncle,

> *I thought that I would write you a few lines to let you know how much trouble we are in. Last Tuesday, Uncle Allen Martin was coming home from the field and stopped to let his horse drink water and while he was there Willy Bunn was behind some bushes and shot him down. It didn't kill him dead at first, but he died in a short time afterwards. Dora was the first one that went to him. When she got to him she said papa what can I do for you? Anything? He looked up at her like he knew her, but he could not speak.*

The Negro shot one eye out, a shot went in his forehead, and two or three others went in his face. The men have been hunting for Willy ever since. They caught the Negro that let him have the gun and put him in jail; he is Mose Ware eldest son. The Negro who shot him has been living on his place nearly six years. It is supposed that it arose from school meeting. Jim Ware, the Negro that gave the gun, ran for school director but Uncle Allen was elected and it made the Negroes mad.

Uncle Allen was getting along well. He was out of debt and had enough money to run him this year. He has a fine crop if it will rain now--will make fine corn and cotton. I haven't any more news to write so I will close. Your niece, Alice Martin.

The court records from the trial of Bunn reveal he was not normal mentally and had lived on the farm as stated in the letter. Mr. Martin had told him he would deed him "a little land for his own." The boy's friends told him, "no white man would ever do that," which riled him. After he was caught, he kept saying, "I shot the best friend I've ever had." He was found guilty, but before he could be sentenced, he was lynched from the oak tree that still stands in front of the Calhoun County courthouse.

II.1.D.A.5.I. (1) MINK MARTIN (B. 1875 CALHOUN COUNTY, AR)

Parents: James Allen Martin and Loula West
   1880 census: Calhoun County, AR in the residence of her father and stepmother.
   Mink was never married as she cared for her younger brother, Jimmy, who was an invalid from birth.

II.1.D.A.5.I. (2) DORA MARTIN (B. 1878 AR)

Parents: James Allen Martin and Lucinda Hanna
   1880 census: Calhoun County, AR in the residence of her parents.
   1930 census: Calhoun County, AR with spouse, Murry. They owned their house valued at $2500 and his occupation was listed as a retail merchant. Their year of marriage is estimated as 1905. The couple had no children through the 1930 census. Murry was sheriff of Calhoun County, AR 1911-1916.

II.1.D.A.5.I. (3) JAMES E. MARTIN (B. 1881 CALHOUN COUNTY, AR)

Parents: James Allen Martin and Lucinda Hanna

Two nicknames: "Jimmy" and "Bud"

He never married and was cared for by his sister Mink, as he was an invalid from birth.

II.1.D.A.5.J. MITCHELL CHESLEY MARTIN (10 AUGUST 1853 COWETTA COUNTY, GA- 11 NOVEMBER 1897 CLAY COUNTY, AL)

Parents: James Franklin Martin and Margaret Walker

Spouse: Martha Ann McCormick (b. 1859)

Children: William Sanders, James Henry, Eliza Ann, Wyatt Washington, and Chesley Allen.

Mitchell is interred in New Harmony Christian Church cemetery in Clay County, AL.

William Sanders Martin (b. February 1884 Clay County, AL)

James Henry Martin (b. January 1886 Clay County, AL) Spouse: Emma Peters. Some researchers report he moved to Oklahoma.

Eliza Ann Martin (b. May 1888 Clay County, AL) Spouse: Glover McCain Wyatt Washington Martin (27 November 1890 Clay County, AL-April 1964 Oklahoma)

Chesley Allen Martin (6 June 1894 Clay County, AL-June 1973 Carter, Oklahoma) There are some research notes indicating he and his wife operated a bakery at Cedartown, GA in the 1940s.

II.1.D.A.5.K. ELIZABETH MARTIN (15 APRIL 1858 TALLADEGA COUNTY, AL- 12 MARCH 1943 CLAY COUNTY, AL)

Parents: James Franklin Martin and Margaret Walker

1930 census: Clay County, AL – Elizabeth is in the residence of her son, Eric.

She married William Mosely Farrow (27 December 1843 Troup County, GA-12 April 1928 Clay County, AL) 11 May 1880 in Clay County, AL.

Children: James B., William Sanders, Kay, Hunter, Eula I., Beatrice, and Eric B.

II.1.d.a.5.k. (1) James B. Farrow (10 May 1881 Clay County, AL-16 July 1946 Clay County, AL)

Parents: William Mosely Farrow and Elizabeth Martin

In the 1920 census, he was in Clay County, AL with spouse, Arie, and son, Emil (25 February 1908 Clay County, AL-August 1977 Clay County, AL). An occupation was not listed for him. In the 1930 census, the family remained intact at the same location with their occupation listed as farming. Their estimated year of marriage was 1906.

II.1.d.a.5.k. (2) William Sanders Farrow (b. December 1884 Clay County, AL)

Parents: William Mosely Farrow and Elizabeth Martin

William is found in the 1930 census living in Randolph County, AL in the Fox Creek community. The census image was too dark to determine any additional information.

II.1.d.a.5.k. (3) Kay Farrow (16 January 1886 Clay County, AL-27 April 1957 Clay County, AL)

Parents: William Mosely Farrow and Elizabeth Martin

II.1.d.a.5.k. (4) Eula I. Farrow (January 1890 Clay County, AL-01 May 1950 Clay County, AL)

Parents: William Mosely Farrow and Elizabeth Martin

In 1930, she resided in Clay County, AL with spouse, George O. Miller (1883 AL-26 May 1950 Clay County, AL), and three daughters. Pauline and Mary were two daughters' names and the oldest daughter's name is unreadable. From the census, Pauline's year of birth is estimated as 1916, and Mary's year of birth as 1925. Their occupation was farming.

II.1.d.a.5.k. (5) Hunter Farrow (25 December 1888 Clay County, AL-20 July 1967 Clay County, AL)

Parents: William Mosely Farrow and Elizabeth Martin

Hunter resided in Clay County, AL in 1930 with spouse, Laura, and four sons, Taylor (b. 1915 AL), William A. (24 December 1917 AL-2 August 1969 District of Columbia), Marcus (b. 1924 AL) and Freddie (b. 1929 AL). His occupation was listed as farming.

Social Security records show his spouse was Laura Jane East (25 August 1891 Pike County, AL-27 March 1985 Clay County, AL). From the 1930 census, their year of marriage is estimated as 1913.

II.1.d.a.5.k. (6) Beatrice Farrow (b. May 1892 Clay County, AL)

Parents: William Mosely Farrow and Elizabeth Martin

She lived in Clay County, AL in 1930 with her husband, David A. Caldwell (1862-August 1939 Clay County, AL), and daughter, Annie L. (b. 1925 AL). Like her siblings, they were farmers.

II.1.d.a.5.k. (7) Eric B. Farrow (5 April 1895 Clay County, AL-28 March 1967 Clay County AL)

Parents: William Mosely Farrow and Elizabeth Martin

In 1930, Eric resided in Clay County, AL working the family farm. In the residence were his spouse, Ada (15 June 1891 AL-May 1974 Clay County, AL), and mother. There are no children listed in the 1930 census.

II.1.d.a.6 Elizabeth Martin (16 December 1818 Edgefield District SC-8 March 1892 Rusk County, TX)

Parents: John Martin, Jr. and Abigail Freeman

In the 1850 census, she resided in Edgefield County, SC with her husband, Milton, and three children. At that time, only enumerations were done on the census tallies rather than listing the names of each individual family member. The family remained in the same location through the censuses of 1860 and 1870. In the 1880 census, the family had moved to Aiken County, SC. In later censuses, they are located in various parts of Texas.

From her mother's will, Elizabeth married Milton J. Palmer (5 July 1818 Edgefield District SC-12 April 1905 Rusk County TX) as he is named as the administrator. The will also names a bequest to a granddaughter, Martha, wife of Ninean Palmer.

Marriage records from Edgefield County, SC show that Elizabeth and Milton were married on 13 February 1846. Milton's will names nine children: Julia Savannah, McPherson O'Neil, Surrenia Florida, Noreganset Pawtucket, Worcester Herst, Emma Arabella, George Ezra, John Walter, and Zipporah E.

Both Milton and Elizabeth are interred in Black Jack Cemetery in Rusk County, TX.

II.1.D.A.6.A Julia Savannah Palmer (7 April 1846 Edgefield County, SC-3 January 1925 Rusk County, TX)

Parents: Milton J. Palmer and Elizabeth Martin

In the 1920 census, she is located in Rusk County, TX with spouse, George Washington Burton, Sr (17 May 1848 SC-26 January 1933 Rusk County, TX), and son, G.W. Edgefield County, SC records show they were married on 11 November 1869.

George was a member of the Texas state legislature as annotated as his occupation in the 1920 census. According to entries in *Members of the Texas Legislature 1846-1992*, George was a member from Rusk County in the 34th Legislature (1915), the 35th Legislature (1917) and the 36th Legislature (1919). His legislative biography documents a second son of this couple, John D.

He and Julia are both interred in Black Jack Cemetery in Rusk County.

II.1.D.A.6.A (1) George Washington Burton, Jr (25 September 1878 SC-29 November 1955 Rusk County, TX)

Parents: George Washington Burton, Sr. and Julia Savannah Palmer

George Jr. chose farming on his family's land as his occupation up until World War I. During the war, he was a sergeant assigned to the 165th Depot Brigade, 35th Company, at Camp Travis TX. Following the war, he returned to the family farm where he remained until his death.

II.1.D.A.6.A (2) JOHN D. BURTON (16 OCTOBER 1875-2 SEPTEMBER 1960 RUSK COUNTY, TX)

Parents: George Washington Burton, Sr. and Julia Savannah Palmer

Like his brother, George, farming was in his blood. He remained on the family farm, assisting his brother, until his death. Neither George nor John had known wives or children.

II.1.D.A.6.B MCPHERSON O'NEIL PALMER (23 JANUARY 1848 EDGEFIELD SC-23 APRIL 1878 AIKEN COUNTY, SC)

Parents: Milton J. Palmer and Elizabeth Martin

McPherson is interred in Graniteville Cemetery in Aiken County.

II.1.D.A.6.C SURRENIA FLORIDA PALMER (11 JUNE 1849 EDGEFIELD SC-9 JANUARY 1921 RUSK COUNTY, TX)

Parents: Milton J. Palmer and Elizabeth Martin

In 1870, she and her spouse, Eugene B. Cogburn (b. 1846 SC), resided in Edgefield County, SC. In the 1880 census, they are listed with a son, Matthew Eugene. Like other family members, they migrated to Texas were residing in Rusk County by the 1920 census. In 1920, Eugene's occupation was listed as nursery agent.

Eugene enlisted on the Confederate side of the Civil War in Company K, 5th South Carolina Reserves, with the rank of private. He and Surrenia were wed after his military service on 10 December 1869 in Edgefield County.

II.1.D.A.6.C (1) MATTHEW EUGENE COGBURN (1877 SOUTH CAROLINA-26 MARCH 1964 CHEROKEE COUNTY, TX)

Parents: Eugene B. Cogburn and Surrenia Florida Palmer

The first census where Matthew is listed living apart from his parents is in 1930. In that year, he resided in Cherokee County, TX with spouse, Minnie V., and worked as a grocery merchant. Their year of marriage is estimated as 1895.

II.1.D.A.6.D NOREGANSET PAWTUCKET PALMER (8 AUGUST 1850 EDGEFIELD SC-27 NOVEMBER 1867)

Parents: Milton J. Palmer and Elizabeth Martin

II.1.D.A.6.E. WORCESTER HERST PALMER (B. 18 JANUARY 1853 EDGEFIELD SC)

Parents: Milton J. Palmer and Elizabeth Martin
He married Mary Ann burton 29 November 1870 in Edgefield County, SC.
In the 1880 census, Worcester lived in Edgefield County, SC with spouse, Mary, and two children, Worcester (b. 1879 SC) and Minnie (b. 1871 SC). His occupation was farming.
The next census listing is not until 1930 where Mary is found in York County, SC, age 79, and annotated as widowed.

II.1.D.A.6.F EMMA ARABELLA PALMER (11 OCTOBER 1853 EDGEFIELD SC-2 MAY 1941)

Parents: Milton J. Palmer and Elizabeth Martin
She married William B. Green (10 May 1855 SC-15 January 1913 Aiken County, SC) on 15 January 1880 in Edgefield County, SC. No children have been located for this couple. Both William and Emma are interred in Graniteville Cemetery in Aiken County, SC.

II.1.D.A.6.G GEORGE EZRA PALMER (15 NOVEMBER 1855 EDGEFIELD SC-4 SEPTEMBER 1901 RUSK COUNTY, TX)

Parents: Milton J. Palmer and Elizabeth Martin
There are no census listings of this couple. By the time of the 1920 census, George has died and his widow, Martha Cumile Woolverton (17 September 1853 Rusk County, TX-8 March 1947), resided in Rusk County, TX with three children, Maud R., Henry and Mary J. In 1930, Martha, Maud and Mary remained in Rusk County.
Maud R. (b. 1892 TX), in both 1920 and 1930, worked in retail sales. Henry (b. 1894 TX) in the 1920 census, was annotated as teamster, long wagon. A 1930 census listing was not found for him. Mary J. (b. 1897 TX) did not have an occupation listed in 1920. Her occupation, in 1930 was listed as a telephone operator.

II.1.D.A.6.H JOHN WALTER PALMER (B. 30 OCTOBER 1857 EDGEFIELD SC)

Parents: Milton J. Palmer and Elizabeth Martin

He married Eliza Fowler on 8 October 1887 in Edgefield County, SC. John Walter is interred in Graniteville Cemetery in Aiken County, SC.

II.1.D.A.6.I ZIPPORAH E. PALMER (18 MARCH 1860 EDGEFIELD SC-20 DECEMBER 1926)

Parents: Milton J. Palmer and Elizabeth Martin

She married Lewis Jackson on 7 November 1875 in Edgefield County, SC. In 1880, Zipporah resided in Aiken County, SC with her spouse, Lewis.

II.1.D.B WILLIAM MARTIN, SR. (1783 SC-12 JUNE 1855 GREENE COUNTY, AL)

Parents: John Martin, Sr and Unity Nancy Barksdale

In the 1850 census, William is found in Greene County, AL with a spouse, Margaret McCarter (1791 SC-26 November 1856 Greene County, AL).

From *Abstracts of Old Ninety-Six and Abbeville District Wills and Bonds*:

> *On April 25, 1803 William Martin received from John Martin, Sr the sum of 14 lb. and 13 shillings as his share from his grandfather, John Barksdale deceased.*

He and Margaret had 12 children: William, James, John, Sarah Caroline, Pharis, Nancy Emmeline, Robert, Marshall, Margaret Elizabeth, Edward, Catherine, and Martha M. The names were discovered through examination of family estate documents on file in the South Carolina State Museum and Archives in Columbia and Camden.

II.1.D.B.1 WILLIAM MARTIN, JR. (1807 SC-6 DECEMBER 1855 GREENE COUNTY, AL)

Parents: William Martin Sr. and Margaret McCarter

He was married first to Gustian Horne and second to Julia Newcomb. He and Gustian had one child, Margaret A.E. He and Julia had nine children.

John H.
Leona Josephine
William H.
Thomas E. (b. abt. 1840)
Narcissa C. (b. abt. 1842)
Francis M. (b. abt. 1844)
Emily Caroline (b. abt. 1845)
Christopher Columbus (b. abt. 1850)
Mary Elizabeth (b. abt. 1851)

II.1.D.B.2 JAMES MARTIN (1809 ABBEVILLE SC-28 APRIL 1859 GREENE COUNTY, AL)

Parents: William Martin, Sr. and Margaret McCarter
   James was first married to Elizabeth Williams on 6 January 1831 in Greene County, AL. They had three children: William R., James F., and John T. He married second, Katherine McMillan on 23 May 1839 in Greene County, AL. They had one daughter, Martha Jane.

II.1.D.B.2.A WILLIAM R. MARTIN (ABT. 1833 GREENE COUNTY, AL-21 OCTOBER 1901)

Parents: James Martin and Elizabeth Williams

II.1.D.B.2.B JAMES F. MARTIN (1836 GREENE COUNTY, AL-17 SEPTEMBER 1889)

Parents: James Martin and Elizabeth Williams

II.1.D.B.2.C JOHN T. MARTIN (30 OCTOBER 1831 GREENE COUNTY, AL-20 APRIL 1891)

Parents: James Martin and Elizabeth Williams
   In the 1880 census, we find he and his spouse, Nancy, and two children, Julia (b. 1867 AL) and Lewis G. (b. 1870 AL), residing in Hale County, AL.

II.1.D.B.2.D MARTHA JANE MARTIN (B. 1848 GREENE COUNTY, AL)

Parents: James Martin and Katharine McMillan

II.1.D.B.3 JOHN MARTIN (27 MAY 1810 SC-6 NOVEMBER 1859 GREENE COUNTY, AL)

Parents: William Martin, Sr. and Margaret McCarter

John was married first to Nancy Peterson on 12 December 1834 in Greene County, AL. They had five children: Mary A.E., Frances E., Julia Ann, Margaret, and John H.F.

He next married Bathsheba Hester on 14 October 1846. They had six children: Elsa L., Martha Olena, Indiana F., Luetta L., Susan and Adline H.

II.1.D.B.3.A MARY A.E. MARTIN (1836 GREENE COUNTY, AL-05 JANUARY 1914 LAWRENCE COUNTY, AL)

Parents: John Martin and Nancy Peterson
Spouse: Samuel W. McRight

II.1.D.B.3.B FRANCES E. MARTIN (B. 1837 GREENE COUNTY, AL)

Parents: John Martin and Nancy Peterson
Spouse: John B. Crawford

II.1.D.B.3.C JULIA ANN MARTIN (1839 GREENE COUNTY, AL-1901)

Parents: John Martin and Nancy Peterson
Spouse: Jesse M. Melton

II.1.d.b.3.d Margaret Martin (b. 1842 Greene County, AL)

Parents: John Martin and Nancy Peterson
    Spouse: James Pinkney Rice
James served in Company I, 20th Alabama Infantry, with the rank of private during the Civil War.

II.1.d.b.3.e John H.F. Martin (b. 1845 Greene County, AL)

Parents: John Martin and Nancy Peterson
    Spouse: H.P. Cobb

II.1.d.b.3.f Elsa L. Martin (b. 1847 Greene County, AL)

Parents: John Martin and Bathsheba Hester

II.1.d.b.3.g Martha Olena Martin (1849 Greene County, AL-1896)

Parents: John Martin and Bathsheba Hester
    Martha resided in Houston County, TX in 1880 with husband, John Daniel Hartgraves (b. 1846 TX), and children, Lee F. (b. 1868 TX), William (b. 1872 TX), John (b. 1873 TX) and Asa E. (b. 1875 TX).
    John served in Company H, 7th Texas Calvary, during the Civil War with the rank of private. On 02 September 1879, he was given 50.20 acres of land, and his annotated occupation in 1880 was farming.

II.1.d.b.3.h Indiana Martin (1851 Greene County, AL-1893)

Parents: John Martin and Bathsheba Hester
    Spouse: Gene Hart

II.1.d.b.3.i Luetta L. Martin (b. 1853)

Parents: John Martin and Bathsheba Hester

II.1.d.b.3.j Susan Martin (1856-1922)

Parents: John Martin and Bathsheba Hester
    Spouse: John Reuben Hairston

II.1.d.b.3.k Adline H. Martin (b. 1859)

Parents: John Martin and Bathsheba Hester
    Spouse: Andrew Sanders

II.1.d.b.4 Sarah Caroline Martin (1815 Abbeville SC-25 June 1887 Hale County, AL)

Parents: William Martin, Sr. and Margaret McCarter
    She married Peter P. Stokes (28 September 1806 SC-7 October 1871 Perry County, AL) on 4 January 1833 in Greene County, AL.

In 1850, they lived in Greene County, AL and had 11 children. Peter was a real estate farmer.

William M. (b. 1835 AL)

Rachel Elizabeth (b. 1836 AL)

Mary Martha (1838 Greene County, AL-1868 Perry County, AL). She married William Mathis Pool (30 October 1835 Perry County, AL-1913 Grimes County, TX). Mary Martha died in childbirth leaving no children. William later remarried to Mary's sister, Martha Rebecca.

Robert (b. 1839 Greene County, AL)

William B. (b. 1840 Greene County, AL)

James D. (b. 1842 Greene County, AL). James served in Company B, 38th Alabama Infantry, at the rank of private during the Civil War.

Emeline (b. 1843 Greene County, AL)

Timen P. (b. 1845 Greene County, AL)

Catharine A. (b. 1847 Greene County, AL). She married John W. Hagood on 17 September 1866 in Jefferson County, AL.

Martha Rebecca (1848 Greene County, AL-16 June 1923). Martha Rebecca married William Mathis Pool on 16 January 1869. In 1880, she, William and four children are listed in the census at Milam County, TX. The page had weathered and the children's names are not readable. Grubaugh documents the couple had four daughters and three sons.

William Mathis served in Company D, 24th Alabama Regiment, from 24 January 1862-1 May 1865 as a private during the Civil War. He is interred in Steele's Grove Cemetery in Erwin, Texas.

Amanda J. (b. April 1850 Greene County, AL)

Peter and Sarah are interred in Stokes Cemetery in Hale County, AL.

II.1.D.B.5. PHARIS MARTIN (B. ABT. 1817 SC)

Parents: William Martin, Sr. and Margaret McCarter

In the 1850 census, he, his spouse, Rebecca Stokes (b. 1813 SC), and two daughters lived in Greene County, AL. Their year of marriage is estimated to be 1840. Children: Margaret E. (b. 1845 Greene County, AL) and Mary C. (b. 1848 Greene County)

II.1.D.B.6. NANCY EMMELINE MARTIN (ABT. 1821 SC-BETWEEN 1870 AND 1880)

Parents: William Martin, Sr. and Margaret McCarter

She married Drury "Drew" E. King (b. 1814 AL) on 26 February 1845 in Greene County, AL.

In the 1850 census, Nancy resided in Greene County, AL with her spouse, Drury, and three children, Martha E, Sarah Catherine and John W. Their occupation is listed as farmers. Alabama land records show that 40 acres were granted to her spouse on 1 March 1850. By the 1870 census, the family has moved to Hale County, AL and added a son, Robert L. In the 1880 census, Drury resided with his daughter, Martha, in Hale County and was widowed. In that census, his occupation is listed as fisherman.

II.1.D.B.6.A MARTHA E. KING (1846 AL-MARCH 1934 SHELBY COUNTY, AL)

Parents: Drury E. King and Nancy Emmeline Martin

The first census where Martha is not in her parents' residence is 1880. In that year, she resided in Hale County, AL with spouse, Benjamin Stevens (1836 AL-29 July 1912 Mobile, AL), two children and two stepchildren. Their occupation was farming. By 1920, she was widowed and lived in Lee County, AL.

Children: Nancy E. (b. 1876) and William Z. (b. February 1880).

Benjamin Stevens had two children from his first marriage: Elizabeth and Martha S.

II.1.d.b.6.b Sarah Catherine King (b. 1848 AL)

Parents: Drury E. King and Nancy Emmeline Martin

Other than the 1850-1870 census listings where Sarah resided with her parents, no other data has been located for her.

II.1.d.b.6.c John W. King (May 1850 AL– June 1939 Hale County, AL)

Parents: Drury E. King and Nancy Emmeline Martin

In 1880, John and his brother, Robert, lived in Hale County, AL. They were tenant farmers. After that year, no other census listings are found for John. However, his death certificate is available from the Alabama Vital Statistics Bureau.

II.1.d.b.6.d Robert L. King (b. 1859 AL)

Parents: Drury E. King and Nancy Emmeline Martin

Robert lived with his brother, John, in 1880. His occupation was farm laborer.

II.1.d.b.7 Robert Martin (b. abt. 1821 SC)

Parents: William Martin, Sr. and Margaret McCarter

He married Letitia McMillan in 1843 in Greene County, AL.

In the 1850 census, Robert Martin resided in Greene County, AL with spouse, Letitia, and their first four children. They remained in the same location in 1860 with seven children in the household. Their daughter, Margaret, was no longer listed with the family in 1860. By 1870, the family had moved to Hale County, AL and all the children except for the oldest three were in the residence. Their occupation was listed as farmers. They remained in Hale County through the 1880 census with the youngest five children in the house. Their children were:

John W.

Margaret A.

Francis Edward

James M.

Kissiah
Pinkney
Mary
Peterson
Benjamin E.
Frederick H.

II.1.d.b.7.a John W. Martin (b. 1844 Greene County, AL)

Parents: Robert Martin and Letitia McMillan
    1850 census: Greene County, AL in parents' residence
    1860 census: Greene County, AL in parents' residence
    1880 census: Hale County, AL with spouse, Mary L., and three children: Robert H. (b. 1866 AL), Margaret A. (b. 1869 AL) and Wade H. (b. 1872 AL). His occupation was a miller.

II.1.d.b.7.b Margaret A. Martin (b. 1845 Greene County, AL)

Parents: Robert Martin and Letitia McMillan
    Following the 1850 census, no additional information has been found for Margaret.

II.1.d.b.7.c Francis Edward Martin (b. 1847 Greene County, AL)

Parents: Robert Martin and Letitia McMillan
    1880 census: Hale County, AL with spouse, Melissa A., and three children: William T. (b. 1872 AL), Ella (b. 1876 AL) and Martha E. (b. 1879 AL). His occupation was a farmer.

II.1.d.b.7.d James M. Martin (b. 1849 Greene County, AL)

Parents: Robert Martin and Letitia McMillan
    Although he resided in his parents' residence in 1870, James worked as a laborer on a neighboring farm. By 1880, James had married and changed occupations to miller. His spouse in the 1880 census is listed as Martha A. There were no children listed in the household.

II.1.D.B.7.E KISSIAH MARTIN (B. 1852 AL)

Parents: Robert Martin and Letitia McMillan

Beyond the three census listings in the years 1860-1880 where Kissiah resided in her parents' residence, no additional data has been found for her.

II.1.D.B.7.F PINKNEY MARTIN (B. 1854 AL)

Parents: Robert Martin and Letitia McMillan

Pinkney is listed in his parents' household 1860-1870. Census listings beyond 1870 were not located.

II.1.D.B.7.G MARY MARTIN (B. 1856 AL)

Parents: Robert Martin and Letitia McMillan

1860 census: Greene County, AL in parents' residence.

1870 and 1880 censuses: Hale County, AL in parents' residence.

II.1.D.B.7.H PETERSON MARTIN (B. 1858 AL)

Parents: Robert Martin and Letitia McMillan

By 1880, Peterson had married and lived in Hale County, AL with spouse, Julia E., and two children, Annie D (b. 1878 AL) and Mary (b. December 1879 AL). His occupation was farmer.

II.1.D.B.7.I BENJAMIN E. MARTIN (B. 1859 AL)

Parents: Robert Martin and Letitia McMillan

Benjamin lived with his parents through the 1880 census. In 1920, he lived in Lee County, AL with spouse, Ollie (1868 AL-02 March 1945 Hale County, AL), and five children. They operated a cotton mill. Their children were:

Ruth (b. 1899 AL), in 1920, worked in the family's cotton mill.

Charlie (b. 1903 AL) also worked in the family's cotton mill.

Paul J. (29 January 1905 AL-May 1985 Jefferson County, AL) married Veria M. in 1927. In 1930, the couple lived in Jefferson County, AL and Paul was employed as a streetcar motorman.

John (b. 1906 AL)
Mack (b. 1908 AL)

II.1.d.b.7.j FREDERICK H. MARTIN (B. 1862 AL)

Parents: Robert Martin and Letitia McMillan
He remained in his parents' residence through the 1880 census. After that year, no additional data has been located for him.

II.1.d.b.8 MARSHALL MARTIN (20 SEPTEMBER 1823 GREENE COUNTY, AL-9 SEPTEMBER 1889 HALE COUNTY, AL)

Parents: William Martin, Sr. and Margaret McCarter
In the 1860 census, Marshall lived in Greene County, AL with spouse, Elizabeth, and three children. The only readable child's name from that census is Nancy. His occupation was farmer.

II.1.d.b.9 MARGARET ELIZABETH MARTIN (ABT. 1827 SC-28 JULY 1906 HALE COUNTY, AL)

Parents: William Martin, Sr. and Margaret McCarter
No records exist of a spouse or children.

II.1.d.b.10 EDWARD MARTIN (B. ABT. 1828 SC)

Parents: William Martin, Sr. and Margaret McCarter
In 1850, Edward lived in Greene County, AL with spouse, Sarah, and newborn son, William (b. January 1850 Greene County, AL). His and Sarah's estimated year of marriage was 1849. He lived next door to his parents and no occupation was listed.

II.1.d.b.11 CATHERINE MARTIN (ABT. 1833 GREENE COUNTY, AL-AFTER 1860)

Parents: William Martin, Sr. and Margaret McCarter
  Catherine married John Parr on 19 May 1857 in Greene County, AL.
  In the 1860 census, she lived in Greene County, AL with spouse, John, and son, William H. (b. 1858 AL). Their occupation was listed as farmers. By 1870, Catherine is no longer found, but John is located in Hale County, AL married to a different person and has six children including William. It has been reported by other researchers that Catherine died after 1860. It is impossible to know which of the other five children annotated in the 1870 census belonged to Catherine, if any, and which were born of John's second marriage.

II.1.d.b.12 MARTHA M. MARTIN (B. 1835 GREENE COUNTY, AL)

Parents: William Martin, Sr. and Margaret McCarter
  She married Anthony C. Baker on 14 December 1853 in Greene County, AL.

II.1.d.c. POLLY A.K.A. MARY MARTIN (3 JULY 1784 EDGEFIELD DISTRICT, SC-7 JANUARY 1859 ABBEVILLE DISTRICT, SC)

Parents: John Martin, Sr and Unity Nancy Barksdale
  1810 census: Abbeville, SC
  1820 census: Edgefield, SC
  1830 census: Abbeville, SC
  She married James Freeman (12 December 1777 Edgefield County, SC-1845 Abbeville, SC) on 8 September 1802 in Abbeville.
  They had eight children: Littleberry B., Henry, Sterling, Caroline, Frances, Celia, Mary Ann and Charles M.
  On April 25, 1803, James Freeman received $187.25, his wife's legacy, from the estate of her grandfather, John Barksdale. (John Barksdale's will is on file at South Carolina State Archives and History in Columbia, Box 105, Pack 2666)
  James Freeman died intestate, meaning he left no will. James F. Martin brought a bill for partition in Equity Court of Edgefield District, SC against L.B. Freeman (son of James Freeman) and Chesley Wells (spouse of Caroline Freeman) on 24 September 1845. The court awarded half of the proceeds of the sale of the estate to James F. Martin, 3/8ths to L.B. Freeman and 1/8 to Chesley Wells. (Woodson)

II.1.d.c.1 Littleberry B. Freeman

Parents: James Freeman and Polly Martin

Other than the mention of him as a defendant in the settlement of his father's estate in 1845, no other records have been located on this gentleman.

II.1.d.c.2 Henry Freeman

Parents: James Freeman and Polly Martin

Other than for his mention as a party of interest in the settlement of his father's estate in 1845, no other records have been located on this gentleman.

II.1.d.c.3 Sterling Freeman (b. 1819 SC)

Parents: James Freeman and Polly Martin

    1820 census: Edgefield, SC in parents' residence.

    1830 census: Abbeville, SC in parents' residence.

    1850 census: Edgefield, SC.

    1880 census: Abbeville, SC with spouse, Elizabeth, and no children.

During the Civil War, Sterling served in Company D, 1st South Carolina State Troops, with the rank of private.

II.1.d.c.4 Caroline Freeman (b. 1808 SC)

Parents: James Freeman and Polly Martin

    1810 census: Abbeville SC in parents' residence.

    1820 census: Edgefield SC in parents' residence.

    1830 census: Abbeville SC in parents' residence.

    1870 census: Edgefield SC with spouse, Chesley. This census listed one male child, older than 21 years old, living in the residence. They owned land worth $2100 and personal property worth $475. Their occupation was farming.

II.1.D.C.5 FRANCES FREEMAN (1824 SC-1858 SC)

Parents: James Freeman and Polly Martin

    1830 census: Abbeville, SC in parents' residence.

    1840 census: Edgefield, SC in parents' residence.

    1850 census: Edgefield, SC with spouse, Landon Tucker, Jr. (24 April 1816 SC-01 October 1900 SC), and no children.

    Landon served in Company C, 1st Infantry Regiment, South Carolina during the Civil War with the rank of private. He remarried after the death of Frances.

II.1.D.C.6 CELIA FREEMAN

Parents: James Freeman and Polly Martin

    Spouse: William Crawford

    The only records of Celia's existence are in the case filed in Edgefield District, SC Equity Court by James F. Martin against the intestate of James Freeman in 1845. In the petition, Celia and her spouse were named as parties of interest.

II.1.D.C.7 MARY ANN FREEMAN (B. 1805 SC)

Parents: James Freeman and Polly Martin

    1810 census: Abbeville SC in parents' residence.

    1820 census: Edgefield SC in parents' residence.

    1830 census: Abbeville SC in parents' residence.

    1850 census: Edgefield, SC with spouse, James L. Harrison, and five children. Those children were:

John E. (b. 1832 SC)

George A. (b. 1834 SC)

William H. (b. 1837 SC)

Thomas (b. 1839 SC)

Charles (b. 1841 SC)

Both Mary Ann and James were named as parties of interest in the 1845 petition filed in Edgefield Equity Court concerning the estate of her father.

II.1.D.C.8 CHARLES M. FREEMAN (22 JANUARY 1807 SC-24 JANUARY 1871 ABBEVILLE SC)

Parents: James Freeman and Polly Martin

    1810 census: Abbeville SC in parents' residence.

    1820 census: Edgefield SC in parents' residence.

    1850 census: Edgefield SC with spouse, Cynthia Harmon (1809 SC-1866 McCormick County, SC), and three children.

    Children of Charles and Cynthia:

    1) James Thomas (12 April 1829-4 June 1858). He is interred in the McCormick, SC cemetery.

    2) Alonzo M. (17 July 1836-14 November 1858). He died of typhoid fever and is interred in the McCormick, SC cemetery.

    3) William M. (1838-1862). He is interred in the McCormick, SC cemetery.

    4) Mary Freeman (12 March 1827 Abbeville, SC-8 October 1869 Abbeville, SC). She married Francis Pickens Wells.

    5) Frances Freeman married Rev. George Creighton.

    The year following Cynthia's death, Charles married a second time to Fannie Willis (20 December 1842 SC-12 August 1937 Abbeville, SC) in 1867. The story goes that Fannie could not have children of her own and the couple adopted a child in the first year of their marriage. The name given to the child was Charles Freeman, Jr. (2 February 1868-4 October 1916).

    Charles Freeman, Sr. had a disagreement with a local McCormick, SC church and its pastor. He built his own church and hired a minister, Rev. Creighton, then started the local cemetery where most of the family is buried. Rev. Creighton later married Frances Freeman, the youngest daughter. (Wood 1982, pp. 117-118)

II.1.D.D. SALLY MARTIN (B. 1785 SC)

Parents: John Martin, Sr and Unity Nancy Barksdale

    She married Isaac Israel Davids in 1803.

    Barksdale (1940, p. 73) makes one mention of this couple and refers to John Sr's will with a bond of $5,000.

    On September 30, 1805, Isaac Davids received $391 as his wife's, Sally Davids', part of the estate of her grandfather, John Barksdale. (John Barksdale's will on file at South Carolina State Archives and History in Columbia, Box 105, Pack 2666)

    This ends the lineage of Unity Nancy Barksdale, daughter of John Hickerson Barksdale and Mary Anne Kinkaid, granddaughter of William Barksdale II and Sarah Collier.

CHAPTER 11

II.1.E. RICHARD BARKSDALE (D. CIRCA 27 JUL 1801)

Parents: John Hickerson Barksdale and Mary Anne Kinkaid

Richard was the fifth child and third son of John Hickerson. He served in Pickens' Brigade in the Revolutionary War and was under the command of Col. Anderson in 1779 and 1780 (Moss, 1985).

In the first census of the United States in 1790, we find Richard in Abbeville County, South Carolina. At that census, there were two males over 16, one male under 16, two females and four slaves listed in his residence. In the 1800 census, Richard remained in Abbeville County.

In his will, John Hickerson bequeathed to Richard two tracts of land adjoining the Savannah River. One tract was for 300 acres and the other was 200 acres. Richard was also bequeathed a Negro man named James.

Based upon his will, Capt Barksdale places Richard's death circa 27 July 1801. His estate was granted to Mary Ann Barksdale. Registered marriages of the Ninety-Six and Abbeville Districts of South Carolina confirm that a Richard Barksdale and Mary Ann Martin were married. However, a year was not given. The following names were also mentioned in Richard's will: John, Allen, Higgerson and Higgarson Barksdale, Senior. There is no documentary evidence that the names of those males were his children.

CHAPTER 12

II.1.F. POLLY BARKSDALE (D. CIRCA 1814)

Parents: John Hickerson Barksdale and Mary Anne Kinkaid

Polly was the sixth child and third daughter of John Hickerson. She married first, Robert Carter, in Charlotte County, VA on 26 November 1774. Her second spouse had the surname Sharp.

In her father's will, she was referred to as Patty with surnames of Carter and Sharp. He bequeathed her one Negro woman named Sarah and one girl named Hannah.

In the Abbeville County, South Carolina archives (box 104; pack 2643) there is a will of an estate of a Polly Barksdale. The will's probate date is 22 March 1814, administered by a Samuel Saxon. However, there is no documentation of what the property consisted of or the heirs. It would be difficult to surmise that this will belonged to Polly, the daughter of John Hickerson and Mary Anne Barksdale. One would assume that her estate would be filed under one of her married names.

Nothing new has been learned about Polly Barksdale since Capt Barksdale's book was published in 1940.

CHAPTER 13

II.1.G. FRANCES BARKSDALE (B. 1764)

Parents: John Hickerson Barksdale and Mary Anne Kinkaid

Frances was the seventh child and fourth daughter of John Hickerson. She married John Matheson in Abbeville County, South Carolina in 1798 (Abbeville Marriages 1780-1879, Implied in Equity Records).

Census Data from 1810 sows the household consisted of:

John Matheson – Marion County, South Carolina

one male under 10 years of age

one male 16-26 years of age

one male 26-45 years of age

two females under 10 years of age

two females 10-16 years of age

one female 16-26 years of age

one female 26-45 years of age

one slave

Frances' father bequeathed her one Negro woman named Stepny and a boy named Tom (Barksdale).

From John Hickerson Barksdale's will, Frances and John had at least one child, Maryann. In that will, Maryann is bequeathed one Negro girl named Luce. The census of 1810 indicates there were probably more children, but only a numeration of the household occupants are included in that census.

Finally, Frances' brother, Higgason, bequeathed in his will a tract of land to "my sister Fanney Matheson's children" (Barksdale, p. 75). This further cements the argument that Maryann was not the only child.

CHAPTER 14

II.1.H. HIGGASON OR HICKERSON BARKSDALE (D. CIRCA 1798)

Parents: John Hickerson Barksdale and Mary Anne Kinkaid

Higgason was the youngest child of John Hickerson. His name is found in history to be spelled as both Higgason and Hickerson.

In Barksdale (p. 75), Fanney is listed as the wife of Richard's brother, Hickerson. Hickerson died in 1798 which would have made Fanney a widow and head of household in 1800, provided she remained unmarried.

In his father's will, the name of the heir is listed as Higgason. Bequeathed to Higgason was the family plantation, 200 acres in Georgia, one Negro man named Stephen, and a bed. Along with Richard, Higgason is named as an executor of the estate.

As best as can be ascertained from existing records, Higgason left Fanney one third part of his estate during her life. The will went on to state that, upon Fanney's death, the estate would go to his brother, Richard. Further, he expressly stated that two Negroes named Mary and Let were to be set free upon his death.

He left to his sister Fanney (Frances) Matheson's children a tract of land. While one may jump to the conclusion that Frances predeceased Higgason, from the census records she was at least alive in 1810. Being that Higgason was the youngest child, one might conclude that Higgason died a relatively young man and expected his sister would predecease him and made provisions for her children.

His will was proved on 2 May 1800 by both Richard and Fanney Barksdale (Abbeville County, Will Book I, pp. 254-55). A few months later it is noted Patty Sharp, sister of deceased, made an application to administer the estate. Mrs. Sharp's application was dated 25 August 1800. The final administration was granted to Fanny Barksdale and George Bowie (Abbeville County Archives, box 5, pack 81).

CHAPTER 15

II.2. HICKERSON BARKSDALE (BIRTH: 1710-1725 TIDEWATER, VA – CIRCA 1797 BUCKINGHAM COUNTY, VA)

Parents: William Barksdale II and Sarah Collier

Because Hickerson's lineage is virtually unknown, as compared to those of his other siblings, he is included as a separate chapter in this book.

Hickerson Barksdale married Bethany Giles (b. 1726 Tidewater, VA). Some sources have the spelling of her given name as Bethania.

Hickerson is the only child of William and Sarah for whom a will has not been located. If he left a will, it would have been destroyed by fire in 1869 when the Buckingham County court house burned.

They lived in the part of Albemarle County that became Buckingham County in 1761. Absence his will, we cannot identify any of the couple's children. In Barksdale's publication, there exists a possibility that three sons existed: Henry, Hickerson and William.

There is a power of attorney, dated in 1839, in which a Henry M. Barksdale of Overton County, Tennessee appointed an agent to collect his wife's estate in Cumberland and Goochland Counties, Virginia (Cumberland County Virginia, Deed Book XXIII, p.468). However, there is no documentary evidence this Henry was the son of Hickerson and Bethany. No evidence corroborates the existence of a third generation male child named Hickerson. There is a William Barksdale documented in Buckingham County as late as 1796, but beyond that, no further trace exists.

Hickerson and Bethany sold 400 acres on Willis Creek to Henry Scruggs and bought 820 acres on the Willis River in present-day Buckingham County in 1760. In 1790, they sold part of the land, 400 acres, to Gulielmus Coleman. (Deed Book 7: 1790-1797 pp. 37 Cumberland County)

Hickerson represented Buckingham County in the Virginia House of Delegates (1783, 1785-87). Found in the records of the Virginia state legislature is a petition dated 29 July 1797 on which Hickerson is a signatory. The petition was to establish a town on the lands of Cut Banks Plantation, owned by Archibald Cary, in Buckingham County, VA near Willis Creek.

In the court records of Buckingham County, Hickerson petitioned for relief from difficult economic conditions on 16 Nov 1789. This was equivalent to filing for bankruptcy today. The petition was granted without prejudice.

Some researchers have reported a date of death for this gentleman as 1794 in Buckingham County, VA. The most telling evidence of his death is found in the LDS Family History Center in Camden, SC. He has a LDS Baptism of 4 June 1943, Endowment 2 Mar 1945, and Sealing Child occurred on 8 Apr 1960. In these records his date of death is undetermined and annotated as after 1794. We will probably never know for sure where and when this gentleman passed. Due to the petition found from the records of the Virginia State Legislature, this history will document his death as after 1797.

CONCLUSION

This edition captures but a small part of the Barksdale family as it starts out in the New World. As followed through the lineage of John Hickerson Barksdale, early ancestors began forging a life for themselves in Virginia, South Carolina, Alabama, Mississippi, Texas and Arkansas. They courageously served their country in the Revolutionary War, the War of 1812, and the Civil War. Some dipped their toes into the political waters of our country and served their communities, states and nation as elected officials. Using their creativeness, they turned resources available to them into entrepreneurial opportunities in agriculture, merchandising, and manufacturing. Some heard a higher calling and faced the moral issues of the time from rural pulpits. Indeed, the early Barksdale ancestors played a vital role in shaping the communities where they settled and the environment into which following generations were born.

Stay tuned for future volumes to come on the remaining descendants of William II: Collier, Thomas Henry, William III, Daniel and Nathaniel.

Appendix 1

Church of Latter Day Saints and Rituals

One of the sources almost all genealogists use is the records of LDS Family History Centers. This work cites LDS ordinances when they are applicable. Therefore, it is important for the reader to understand the relationship of the ordinances to genealogy. The following is a brief and simplified description of those ordinances.

Baptism for the dead by proxy (or "vicarious baptism") is an ordinance practiced by members of the Church of Jesus Christ of Latter-day Saints, some Native American religions, and other Mormon churches. A living person, as a proxy, is baptized by immersion in typical Mormon fashion except the prayer accompanying the baptism states that the baptism is being performed for and in behalf of a deceased person whose name has been submitted for that ordinance.

According to the LDS Church, the Mormons base this practice on a revelation Joseph Smith received and first taught as doctrine at the funeral sermon of LDS member Seymour Brunson. In a letter written on October 19, 1840 to the Quorum of the Twelve Apostles of the LDS Church (who were on a mission in Great Britain at the time), Joseph refers to the passage in 1 Corinthians 15:29 (KJV):

> *I presume the doctrine of "baptism for the dead" has reached your ears, and may have raised some inquiries in your minds respecting the same. I cannot in this letter give you all the information you may desire on the subject; but aside from knowledge independent of the Bible, I would say that it was certainly practiced by the ancient churches; and St. Paul endeavors to prove the doctrine of the resurrection from the same, and says, "Else what shall they do which are baptized for the dead, if the dead rise not at all? Why are they then baptized for the dead?" (Roberts 1902, 4:231)*

Other LDS scripture expands upon this doctrine and commands such baptisms are to be performed in Temples of which there are more than 100 worldwide. The LDS Church holds deceased persons who have not accepted or had the opportunity to accept the faith in this life will have the opportunity to accept the faith in the afterlife, but in order to do so, they must receive all the LDS ordinances including baptism. For this reason, genealogy forms an important basis of research in the LDS Church's efforts to perform temple ordinances for as many deceased persons as possible. As a part of these efforts, a number of high profile people who have had temple ordinances performed on their behalf have received particular attention, including the founding fathers of the U.S., presidents of the U.S., John Wesley, Christopher Columbus, Jewish Holocaust victims, Ghengis Khan, Joan of Arc, Adolf Hitler, Josef Stalin and Buddha. Vicarious baptism does not mean the decedent actually accepts the ordinance performed for him or her. It merely means the decedent **may** accept the ordinance and the benefit which the LDS claims it provides. However, LDS leaders have stated people in the afterlife for whom these ordinances have been performed will rarely reject it.

While LDS members consider it a great service to perform vicarious ordinances for the deceased, some non-members have taken offense to what they see as an arrogant practice. To be sensitive to the issue of vicariously baptizing non-Mormons unrelated to Church members, in recent years the LDS Church has emphasized a policy that, generally, its members should only perform temple ordinances for their own direct ancestors. For example, the LDS Church is in the process of removing sensitive names (such as Jewish Holocaust victims) from its International Genealogical Index. D. Todd Christofferson of the LDS Church's Presidency of the Seventy stated removing the names is an "ongoing, labor intensive process requiring name-by-name research. When the Church is made aware of documented concerns, action is taken. Plans are underway to refine this process."

In harmony with these principles, Latter-day Saints identify their ancestors through family history research, build temples, and, on behalf of their progenitors, perform the ordinances that pertain to exaltation: baptism, confirmation, ordination to the priesthood, washing and anointing, endowment, and sealing. Thus, "we redeem our dead, and connect ourselves with our fathers which are in heaven, and seal up our dead to come forth in the first resurrection...[we] seal those who dwell on earth to those who dwell in heaven" (Smith 1976, pp. 337-38).

This is the chain that binds the hearts of fathers and mothers to their children and the hearts of the children to their parents. And this sealing work "fulfills the mission of Elijah" (Smith, p. 330)

APPENDIX 2

Major Surnames Contained Within This Work

Abernathy
Allen
Barkesdale
Barksdale
Haygood
Hobbie
Martin
Pearson
Smith
Waldrop

REFERENCES:

Barksdale, John A. 1940. *Barksdale Family History and Genealogy with Collateral Lines.* Richmond: William Byrd Press.

Biographical Directory of the United States Congress. Allen, Maryon Pittman. http://bioguide. congress.gov/scripts/biodisplay.pl?index=A000139

Calhoun County ArGenWeb. http://www.rootsweb.ancestry.com/~arcalhou/contents. htm#Contents.

Cecille Maxwell Reynolds, e-mail message to author, June 2003.

Chapman, John A. 1897. *History of Edgefield from the Earliest Settlements to 1897.* Newberry, South Carolina: Elbert H. Hull, Publishers and Printers.

Church of Jesus Christ of Latter-day Saints. http://www.familysearch.org/.

Clay County AlGenWeb. http://www.genrecords.net/alclay/.

Coffee County AlGenWeb. http://www.angelfire.com/al2/coffeecounty/index.html.

Cresswell, Stephen. 2006. *Rednecks, Redeemers, and Race: Mississippi after Reconstruction, 1877-1917.* Jackson: University Press of Mississippi.

Curd, Grace W. 1990. *Historical Genealogy of the Woodsons and Their Connections.* Roanoke, VA: G.W. Curd.

David J. Yost, e-mail message to author, September 2003.

Deborah Boswell, e-mail message to author, March 2003.

Debra Crosby, e-mail message to author, March 2003.

Dorothy Martin Reed, in discussion with the author, April 2003.

Douglas County Sentinel, Douglasville, Georgia: 6 July 1988, Obituary section. Published daily.

Eagle Democrat, Warren, Arkansas: 26 August 1987, Obituary section. Published weekly.

Elba Clipper, Elba, Alabama: 24 November 1977, Obituary section. Published weekly.

Elizabeth Hobbie Davis, in discussion with the author, November 2003.

Encyclopedia of American Biography New Series. Vol. 18. New York and West Palm Beach, FL: The American Historical Society, 1945.

England, Mary P. 1965. *Zimmerman Family History*. Westminster, SC: M.P. England.

Family Finder. http://www.genealogy.com/.

Galveston Daily News, Galveston, Texas: 25 August 1996, Obituary section. Published daily.

Galveston Daily News, Galveston, Texas: 24 February 2003, Obituary section. Published daily.

Gore, Walter M. 1922. *History-Genealogical-Biographical of the Barksdale-DuPont and Allied Families*. New York: American Historical Society.

Grace Martin Henshaw, correspondence to the author with annotations from the *Chesley Burton Martin Family Bible*, June 2003.

Greene County AlGenWeb. http://magnolia.cyriv.com/GreeneAlgenweb/default.asp

Hale County, Alabama Free Public Records Directory. http://publicrecords.onlinesearches.com/AL_Hale.htm

Harlice Carson, in discussion with the author, August 2003.

Historical Records. http://search.ancestry.com/.

Hortense Wood, e-mail message to author, March 2003.

Hubert, Sarah D. 1895. *Genealogy of Part of the Barksdale Family of America*. Atlanta: Franklin Printing and Publishing Company.

Jan Woodard, e-mail message to author, April 2003.

Joanna Davenport, in discussion with the author, September 2003.

John White, e-mail message to author, December 2002.

Karen Grubaugh, e-mail message to author, May 2003.

Keelie Thomason, e-mail message to author, September 2003.

LaGrange Daily News, LaGrange, Georgia: 23 June 1951, Obituary section. Published daily.

Gadsden Times, Gadsden, Alabama: 20 August 1958, Obituary section. Published daily.

Gadsden Times, Gadsden, Alabama: 03 June 1978, News section. Published daily.

Gainesville Sun, Gainesville, FL: 19 October 1987, Obituary section. Published daily.

Galveston Daily News, Galveston, Texas: 24 February 2003, Obituary section. Published daily.

June Underwood, correspondence to the author, September 2003.

Las Vegas Review Journal, Las Vegas, Nevada: 12 March 1990, Obituary section. Published daily.

Levy County Journal, Levy, Florida: 20 September 2001, Obituary section. Published weekly.

Lineville Headlight, Clay County, Alabama: 4 February 1916, Obituary section. Published weekly.

Lineville Headlight, Clay County, Alabama: 28 April 1916, Obituary section. Published weekly.

Malden Press-Merit, Dunklin, Missouri: 18 June 1970, Obituary section. Published daily.

Manchester Star-Mercury, Manchester, Georgia: 5 March 1986, Obituary section. Published weekly.

Martha Dingler Moore, e-mail message to author, July 2003.

Memorial record of Alabama: a concise account of the state's political, military, professional and industrial progress, together with the personal memoirs of many of its people. 2 vols. Madison, WI: Brant & Fuller. 1893.

Miami Herald, Miami, Florida: 24 February 2003, Obituary section. Published daily.

Minden Press-Herald, Shreveport, Louisiana: 26 February 1993, Obituary section. Published daily.

Morris, Aubrey R. 1996. *The Haygood's of Mars Hill*. Alpharetta, GA: A.R. Morris.

Moss, Bobby G. 1985. *Roster of South Carolina Patriots in the American Revolution*. Baltimore: Genealogical Publishing Company.

Northwest Arkansas Times, Fayetteville, Arkansas: 25 August 1992, Obituary section. Published daily.

Owen, Thomas M. 1921. *History of Alabama and Dictionary of Alabama Biography*. Chicago: S.J. Clarke Publishing Co.

Palm Beach Post, West Palm Beach, Florida: 23 August 1980, Obituary section. Published daily.

Pine Bluff Commercial, Pine Bluff, Arkansas: 29 October 1942, Obituary section. Published daily.

Pine Bluff Commercial, Pine Bluff, Arkansas: 30 June 1953, Obituary section. Published daily.

Pine Bluff Commercial, Pine Bluff, Arkansas: 11 August 1992, Obituary section. Published daily.

Pine Bluff Commercial, Pine Bluff, Arkansas: 26 March 1994, Obituary section. Published daily.

Ralph Robinson, e-mail message to author, April 2003.

Robert Smith, e-mail message to author, May 2003.

Roberts, B.H., ed. 1902. *History of the Church of Jesus Christ of Latter-day Saints.* 7 vols. Provo, Utah: BOAP.

Rosemary Phelan Harbin, e-mail message to author, December 2002.

San Antonio Express-News, San Antonio, Texas: 28 June 1992, Obituary section. Published daily.

Sansing, David G. 1999. *The University of Mississippi: A Sesquicentennial History.* Jackson: University Press of Mississippi.

Smith, Joseph Jr. 1976. *Teachings of the Prophet Joseph Smith.* Salt Lake City: Deseret Book Company.

The Anniston Star, Anniston, Alabama: 5 May 1979, Obituary section. Published daily.

The Anniston Star, Anniston, Alabama: 30 December 1981, Obituary section. Published daily.

The Atlanta Constitution, Atlanta: 9 December 1968, Obituary section. Published daily.

The Item, Sumter, South Carolina: 28 April 2000, Obituary section. Published daily.

The Item, Sumter, South Carolina: 25 May 2003, Obituary section. Published daily.

The Valley Times-News, Lanett, Alabama: 10 December 1965, Obituary section. Published daily.

The Valley Times-News, Lanett, Alabama: 25 August 1987, Obituary section. Published daily.

The Valley Times-News, Lanett, Alabama: 19 October 1988, Obituary section. Published daily.

The Valley Times-News, Lanett, Alabama: 27 March 1989, Obituary section. Published daily.

The Valley Times-News, Lanett, Alabama: 12 December 1989, Obituary section. Published daily.

The Valley Times-News, Lanett, Alabama: 7 March 1990, Obituary section. Published daily.

The Valley Times-News, Lanett, Alabama: 24 January 1992, Obituary section. Published daily.

Tony Altman, e-mail message to author, April 2003.

TXGenWeb Project. http://www.txgenweb.org/.

Virginia Genealogical Society Quarterly. Series XXVIII, Vol.2. Richmond: Virginia Genealogical Society. May 1990.

Walter Ware Bass, e-mail message to author, June 2003.

Whisenhunt, Donald W. 1983. *A Chronological History of Smith County*. Smith County, TX: Jack T. Greer Memorial Fund of the Smith County Historical Society.

Who Was Who in America? A component of Who's Who in American History. Vol 3, 1951-1960. Chicago: Marquis Who's Who, 1966.

Who Was Who in America? Vol. 7. Chicago: Marquis Who's Who, 1981.

Who's Who in America? Ed. 40. Chicago: Marquis Who's Who, 1978.

Who's Who in American Law? Ed. 1. Chicago: Marquis Who's Who, 1978.

Who's Who in American Law? Ed. 2. Chicago: Marquis Who's Who, 1979.

Wilbarger, J.W. 1889. *Indian Depredations in Texas*. Austin, Texas: Hutchings.

Wisconsin State Journal, Madison, Wisconsin: 16 August 1973, Obituary section. Published daily.

Wood, L.L. 1982. *Old Families of McCormick County*. Greenville, SC: Greenville Print Company.

Young, Willie P. 1950. *Abstracts of Old Ninety-Six and Abbeville District Wills and Bonds*. Greenville, SC: Greenville Print Company.

CONTRIBUTING ORGANIZATIONS:

Abbeville County, South Carolina Clerk of Probate Court

Alabama Department of Archives and History

Anniston-Calhoun County (Alabama) Public Library

Arkansas History Commission and State Archives

Ashland City (Alabama) Public Library

Betty Hagler Library, Douglas County, Georgia

Calhoun County (Arkansas) Public Library

Chambers County (Alabama) Library

City of San Antonio (Texas) Library, Texana/Genealogy Department

Clay County (Alabama) Historical Society

Cobb Memorial Archives, Chambers County, Alabama

Cumberland County Clerk of the Circuit Court, Cumberland, Virginia

Douglas County (Georgia) Public Library

Dunklin County (Missouri) Library

Edgefield County, South Carolina Clerk of Probate Court

Elba (Alabama) Public Library

Florence-Lauderdale (Alabama) Public Library

Fort Sam Houston National Cemetery

Frazer's Chapel of the Chimes, Warren, Arkansas

Gadsden (Alabama) Public Library

H. Grady Bradshaw Library, Chambers County, Alabama

Halifax County Clerk of the Circuit Court, Halifax, Virginia

Jefferson County (Alabama) Library Cooperative

Kaufman County (Texas) Library

Las Vegas/Clark County (Nevada) Library

Levy County (Florida) Public Library

Lewis Cooper Jr. Memorial Library, Opelika, Alabama

Lineville City (Alabama) Public Library

Members of the Texas Legislature, 1846-1992, 2 vols., Austin: Texas Senate, 1992.

Miami-Dade (Florida) Public Library System

Palm Beach County (Florida) Library System

Prairie Grove (Arkansas) Public Library

Redfield (Arkansas) Public Library

Richmond County Clerk of the Circuit Court

Rusk County (Texas) Library

Sauk City (Wisconsin) Public Library

Scott County (Missouri) Historical & Genealogy Society

South Carolina Department of Archives and History

Southeast Arkansas Regional Library, Warren, Arkansas

Springhill (Louisiana) Library

Sumter County (South Carolina) Library System

Texas State Library and Archives

The Library of Virginia

Thornton Public Library, Thornton, Arkansas

Troup County (Georgia) Archives

Tyler (Texas) Public Library

Union County Arkansas Vital Records, Union County Clerk, El Dorado, Arkansas

University of Alabama, Birmingham

Virginia Historical Society Library

White Hall (Arkansas) Public Library

Index of Names

Martin, Cora Eugenia 25
Martin, David Sanders 108
Martin, Dora 103, 116
Martin, Dorothy Delphne 91
Martin, Douglas K. 31
Martin, Edna E. 30
Martin, Edna Iola 106
Martin, Edward 132
Martin, Elizabeth 117, 119
Martin, Elizabeth Glennie 89
Martin, Eliza Cornelia 112
Martin, Elsa L. 126
Martin, Estelle 101
Martin, Ethel 110
Martin, Eugenia L. 100
Martin, Frances 45
Martin, Frances E. 125
Martin, Francis Edward 130
Martin, Frederick H. 132
Martin, George Chesley 92
Martin, Grace W. 89
Martin, Hattie Viola 106
Martin, Helen Ouida 87
Martin, Henry 20
Martin, Henry Harrison 99
Martin, HenryHobbie 32
Martin, Henry Lucious Waits 112
Martin, Hurley 102
Martin, Indiana 126
Martin, James 124
Martin, James Allen 115
Martin, James Chesley 88
Martin, James E. 117
Martin, James Edwin 75
Martin, James F. 16, 17, 124
Martin, James Franklin 44
Martin, James M. 130
Martin, James Ransom 113
Martin, James Samuel 100
Martin, James Wesley 95

Martin, Jeff M. 28
Martin, Jeter Bell 86
Martin, John 15, 16, 125
Martin, John H.F. 126
Martin, John Jr. 16
Martin, John, Jr. 16
Martin, John Lysle 111
Martin, John Sr. 15
Martin, John T. 124
Martin, John Thomas 95
Martin, John Tyler 115
Martin, John W. 130
Martin, Josephine 32
Martin, Josephine Ardella 25
Martin, Julia Ann 125
Martin, Kissiah 131
Martin, Laura Jane 113
Martin, Lillie Eliza Clementine 109
Martin, Lucius A. 94
Martin, Luetta L. 127
Martin, Lula Bess 114
Martin, Lula Lenora 76
Martin, Lydia Charlotte 108
Martin, Manning 102
Martin, Marcie M. 30
Martin, Margaret 126
Martin, Margaret A. 130
Martin, Margaret Elizabeth 132
Martin, Margaret F. 28
Martin, Marshall 132
Martin, Martha 97
Martin, Martha Jane 125
Martin, Martha Luellen 113
Martin, Martha M. 133
Martin, Martha Olena 126
Martin, Mary 131
Martin, Mary A.E. 125
Martin, Mary Alice 23
Martin, Mary Eliza 27
Martin, Mink 116

Martin, Mitchell Andrew 102
Martin, Mitchell Chesley 117
Martin, Myrtle T. 101
Martin, Nancy Emmeline 128
Martin, Nancy Eunis 30
Martin, Nancy Idella 112
Martin, Nonnie 111
Martin, Nora Ella 28
Martin, Omar 102
Martin, Patsy 17
Martin, Peterson 131
Martin, Pharis 128
Martin, Pinkney 131
Martin, Polly 133
Martin, Randall B. 32
Martin, Robert 129
Martin, Robert Allen 113
Martin, Robert Chesley Jr 92
Martin, Robert Chesley Sr 90
Martin, Robert E. Lee 96
Martin, Robert Ware 87
Martin, Rosa Lee Anna 25
Martin, Ruby 101
Martin, Ruth H. 75
Martin, Sally 136
Martin, Samuel Bud 103
Martin, Sanders M. 104
Martin, Sanders Pheris 96
Martin, Sarah Caroline 127
Martin, Sarah E. 27
Martin, Sarah Frances 30
Martin, Scott F. 32
Martin, Sherman Fielder 31
Martin, Sherman Fielder Jr. 31
Martin, Stephen Marion 29
Martin, Susan 127
Martin, Thomas Henry 74
Martin, Toliver Pinkney 17
Martin, Unity 11
Martin, Walter Alonza 103

Martin, W.H. 101
Martin, William 15, 123
Martin, William Clayton 109
Martin, William Elbert 89
Martin, William Ethridge 110
Martin, William Jr. 123
Martin, William Monroe 25
Martin, William P. 95
Martin, William Pheris 93
Martin, William R. 124
Martin, William Ray 27
Martin, William Samuel 94
Martin, Wyatt Sanders 114
Martin, Zachariah 20
Maryon Pittman Mullins 71
Montgomery Buick Company 35
Moore, Martha Dingler 26
Moseley, William 7

N

Neely, Austin 107
Neely, Betty 107
Neely, Bobby 106
Neely, Burton 108
Neely, Charley 107
Neely, Lee 107
Ninety-Six District 10

O

Oakwood Cemetery 36
Orr, Vergie 114
Orr, Vinnie 114

P

Palmer, Emma Arabella 122
Palmer, George Ezra 122
Palmer, John Walter 123
Palmer, Julia Savannah 120
Palmer, McPherson O'Neil 121
Palmer, Noreganset Pawtucket 122
Palmer, Surrenia Florida 121